Ti

Born in Irela... educated at ... and then privately. He gained a triple First at Oxford and was a Fellow and Tutor at Magdalen College 1925–54. In 1954 he became Professor of Medieval and Renaissance English Literature at Cambridge. He was an outstanding and popular lecturer and had a deep and lasting influence on his pupils.

C. S. Lewis was for many years an atheist, and described his conversion in *Surprised by Joy:* "In the Trinity Term of 1929 I gave in, and admitted that God was God . . . perhaps the most dejected and reluctant convert in all England." It was this experience that helped him to understand not only apathy but active unwillingness to accept religion and, as a Christian writer, gifted with an exceptionally brilliant and logical mind and a lucid, lively style, he was without peer. He also wrote books for children, and some science fiction, besides many works of literary criticism. He died on 22 November 1963, at his home in Oxford.

The Reverend Walter Hooper, an Anglican priest, is the literary advisor to the estate of C. S. Lewis. He lives in Oxford.

C. S. LEWIS

Timeless at Heart

Essays on Theology

EDITED BY
WALTER HOOPER

Fount

An Imprint of HarperCollins*Publishers*

First published in 1987 by Fount Paperbacks
an imprint of HarperCollins Religious,
part of HarperCollins Publishers,
77–85 Fulham Palace Road
Hammersmith, London W6 8JB
This edition reprinted 1991

Printed and bound in Great Britain by
HarperCollins Manufacturing, Glasgow

Contents

Preface

No one will ever say "I *think* I remember meeting C.S. Lewis." I've been certain of this since Lewis took me to my first meeting of the Inklings on 10th June 1963. It was here in Oxford, and within minutes of our gathering with our pints in the front room of The Lamb and Flag even those at nearby tables stopped talking so that they could listen to him. Lewis's talk, rich in ideas, orthodoxy and common sense, was as good as anything I ever expect to hear. But I remember almost as well what he led me to say and the clarity with which he caused me to express it. That isn't boasting. Think of those we've met whose conversation becomes bright and witty in proportion as we've been made to sound dull and stupid. With Lewis you wanted to be at your best, and he always made it possible.

We will soon be commemorating the twenty-fifth anniversary of Lewis's death. During that quarter of a century I've talked and corresponded with many thousands of those who admire his theological books. Most of them weren't even born when Lewis was alive, so there are three generations reading his books now. It seems to me that they enjoy an experience remarkably similar to that of those who knew Lewis. His books are very like his conversation in tone and substance. Anyway, it is the books which continue to make it possible for readers, whether they knew the author or not, to understand the Christian faith and express themselves clearly.

It's a pity that not everyone is happy about this. Lewis's ability to reason well and to write lucidly about Christianity is causing quite a lot of grumbling from some quarters. If anyone's books become very well-known it eventually becomes fashionable to attack him. I think this is partly because when all the good things have been said, debunking is more certain of winning attention. Still, as with most fashions, even debunking can come full circle. Some of the present critics, in their fury, call Lewis "popular", "simple", and "traditional", as if these were quite dreadful qualities.

It is surely of some historical interest that the same three epithets were hurled at Lewis when he was alive. As will be seen from my footnotes, several of the essays in this book were written in response to or led to a controversy. The "Rejoinder to Dr Pittenger" is the most carefully considered and detailed response Lewis ever made to what was an extraordinarily ill-mannered piece of debunking. I remember well the stir that was caused when the Reverend Dr Norman Pittenger's "Apologist versus Apologist: A Critique of C.S. Lewis as 'defender of the faith'" appeared in *The Christian Century* of 1st October 1958. One of Dr Pittenger's charges is that Lewis "is the sophisticate who pretends to be very simple indeed, and if the Church has *said* something is in the Scriptures and is to be believed, he takes that as the last word." Well, yes. It cannot be denied that Lewis thought highly of both the Scriptures and the Church, and there was no pretence at all in his simple belief that the Gospel is "timeless at heart". It was neither necessary nor desirable to include Dr Pittenger's "Critique" in this book because Lewis's "Rejoinder" makes clear what things Dr Pittenger thought Lewis too popular, simple and traditional about.

Now and then even those who should know better get worried that modern people can't "relate to" Lewis's clarity of expression. For example, an American publisher told me recently that he wished he could introduce into Lewis's writings such words as "epistemological", "simplistic", "counter-productive" and "syndrome", as he thinks these could provide a necessary veneer of "updating". But Lewis answered this nonsense in the letter following his "Rejoinder", in which he says, "Any fool can write *learned* language. The vernacular is the real test."

Those of us in the Oxford University C.S. Lewis Society learned a good deal about the cautious acceptance of Lewis's books in one of the many foreign countries where they are in translation. Dr Gisbert Kranz, founder of the German Inklings Society in Aachen, read a paper to the Society on 23rd September 1986. Before mentioning that the lectures at Lewis conferences in Germany are now attended by as many as eight hundred people, Dr Kranz explained why it took so long for Lewis to be accepted in his country:

> The first essay of Lewis to appear in Germany represented a kind of reasoning not much esteemed in Germany. Moreover it was written in so clear a style that it was liable to be suspected of shallowness, for a book that is to impress the German high-brows must be written in a very intricate style full of polysyllabic technical terms and difficult to understand, a blend, say, of Heidegger and Hegel, the two most unreadable philosophers in the world. When two years later the second philosophical essay by Lewis appeared in a German edition, it had to be accompanied by an epilogue defending the simplicity of style in a philosophical book.

Finally, before mentioning the essays in this book, I feel Lewis should be allowed a last word regarding his controversy with Dr Pittenger. During the time I was a member of Lewis's household we discussed both the "Critique" and the "Rejoinder". This led us to consider Our Lord's command "Go ye into all the world and preach the Gospel to every creature." "Would Our Lord have given such a command," Lewis said to me, "if He thought it impossible for anyone to do it?"

It is certainly disheartening to realize how many in the world have still not heard the Gospel. Even so, it's a grand thing that Lewis's defence of the Faith is so clear and memorable that no one is ever likely to say "I *think* I've read something by C.S. Lewis."

Two Fount Paperbacks, *God in the Dock* and *First and Second Things*, have already been taken from a large collection of pieces by C.S. Lewis called *Undeceptions* (1971). All but one of the essays which make up *Timeless at Heart* are derived from the same book. However, most of them had appeared elsewhere before they were brought together as *Undeceptions*.

(1) "Christian Apologetics", published originally in *Undeceptions*, was read to an assembly of Anglican priests and youth leaders at the Carmarthen Conference for Youth Leaders and Junior Clergy during Easter 1945.

(2) "Answers to Questions on Christianity" was first published as a pamphlet by the Electrical and Musical Industries Christian Fellowship in Hayes, Middlesex (1944).

(3) "Why I Am Not a Pacifist" was read to a pacifist society in Oxford in 1940. Lewis made a copy of the manuscript for his former pupil and friend, George Sayer, and I have Mr Sayer to thank for providing me with a reproduction of it. The essay was included in an expanded edition of Lewis's *The Weight of Glory and Other Addresses* published by Macmillan Publishing Co. of New York in 1980. However, this is the first time "Why I Am Not a Pacifist" has been published in Great Britain.

(4) "The Pains of Animals: A Problem in Theology" originally appeared in *The Month*, Vol. CLXXXIX (February 1950), pp. 95–104. I am very grateful to Miss M.F. Matthews for permission to include the late Dr C.E.M. Joad's part of this good-natured dispute.

(5) "The Founding of the Oxford Socratic Club" is my title for Lewis's Preface to *The Socratic Digest*, No. 1 (1942–1943). Lewis was the President of the Oxford Socratic Society from its beginning in 1942 until he went to Cambridge in 1955.

(6) "Religion Without Dogma?" was read to the Socratic Society on 20th May 1946, and was published as "A Christian Reply to Professor Price" in *The Phoenix Quarterly*, Vol. I, No. 1 (Autumn 1946), pp. 31–44. It was then reprinted as "Religion Without Dogma?" in *The Socratic Digest*, No. 4 (1948), pp. 82–94. The "Reply" which I have appended to this essay is Lewis's answer to Miss G.E.M. Anscombe's article "A Reply to Mr C.S. Lewis's Argument that 'Naturalism is Self-refuting'", both of which appeared in issue No. 4 of *The Socratic Digest*. Those who are interested in Miss Anscombe's article will find it reprinted in her *Collected Philosophical Papers*, Vol. II (1981).

(7) "Is Theism Important? A Reply" comes from *The Socratic Digest*, No. 5 (1952), pp. 48–51.

(8) "Rejoinder to Dr Pittenger" is taken from *The Christian Century*, Vol. LXXV (26th November 1958), pp. 1359–61. A number of letters to the editor (all supporting Lewis) appeared in *The Christian Century* (24th December 1958), including a long one from Dr Pittenger. Lewis's reply to it was published under the title "Version Vernacular" in *The Christian Century*, Vol. LXXV (31st December 1958), p. 515.

(9) "Willing Slaves of the Welfare State" was originally published in *The Observer* (20th July 1958), p. 6.

(10) There is, finally, a section of letters on theological topics which Lewis published in various journals.

3 March 1987
Walter Hooper
Oxford

1

Christian Apologetics

(1945)

Some of you are priests and some are leaders of youth organizations.[1] I have little right to address either. It is for priests to teach me, not for me to teach them. I have never helped to organize youth, and while I was young myself I successfully avoided being organized. If I address you it is in response to a request so urged that I came to regard compliance as a matter of Obedience.

I am to talk about Apologetics. Apologetics means of course Defence. The first question is – what do you propose to defend? Christianity, of course: and Christianity as understood by the Church in Wales. And here at the outset I must deal with an unpleasant business. It seems to the layman that in the Church of England we often hear from our priests doctrine which is not Anglican Christianity. It may depart from Anglican Christianity in either of two ways: (1) It may be so "broad" or "liberal" or "modern" that it in fact excludes any real Supernaturalism and thus ceases to be Christian at all. (2) It may, on the other hand, be Roman. It is not, of course, for me to define to you what Anglican Christianity is – I am your pupil, not your teacher. But I insist that wherever you draw the lines, bounding lines must exist, beyond which your doctrine will cease either to be Anglican or to be Christian: and I suggest also that the lines come a great deal sooner than many modern priests think. I think it is your duty to fix the lines clearly in your own minds: and if you wish to go beyond them you must change your profession.

[1] This paper was read to an assembly of Anglican priests and youth leaders of the Church in Wales at Carmarthen during Easter 1945

This is your duty not specially as Christians or as priests but as honest men. There is a danger here of the clergy developing a special professional conscience which obscures the very plain moral issue. Men who have passed beyond these boundary lines in either direction are apt to protest that they have come by their unorthodox opinions honestly. In defence of these opinions they are prepared to suffer obloquy and to forfeit professional advancement. They thus come to feel like martyrs. But this simply misses the point which so gravely scandalizes the layman. We never doubted that the unorthodox opinions were honestly held: what we complain of is your continuing your ministry after you have come to hold them. We always knew that a man who makes his living as a paid agent of the Conservative Party may honestly change his views and honestly become a Communist. What we deny is that he can honestly continue to be a Conservative agent and to receive money from one party while he supports the policy of another.

Even when we have thus ruled out teaching which is in direct contradiction to our profession, we must define our task still further. We are to defend Christianity itself – the faith preached by the Apostles, attested by the Martyrs, embodied in the Creeds, expounded by the Fathers. This must be clearly distinguished from the whole of what any one of us may think about God and Man. Each of us has his individual emphasis: each holds, in addition to the Faith, many opinions which seem to him to be consistent with it and true and important. And so perhaps they are. But as apologists it is not our business to defend *them*. We are defending Christianity; not "my religion". When we mention our personal opinions we must always make quite clear the difference between them and the Faith itself. St Paul has given us the model in 1 Corinthians 7:25: on a certain point he has "no commandment of the Lord" but gives "his judgement". No one is left in doubt as to the difference in *status* implied.

This distinction, which is demanded by honesty, also gives the apologist a great tactical advantage. The great difficulty is to get modern audiences to realize that you are preaching Christianity solely and simply because you happen to think it *true*; they always suppose you are preaching it because you like it or think it good for society or something of that sort. Now a clearly maintained distinction between what the Faith actually says and what you would like it to have said, or what you understand or what you personally find helpful or think probable, forces your audience to realize that you are tied to your data just as the scientist is tied by the results of the experiments; that you are not just saying what you like. This immediately helps them to realize that what is being discussed is a question about objective fact – not gas about ideals and points of view.

Secondly, this scrupulous care to preserve the Christian message as something distinct from one's own ideas, has one very good effect upon the apologist himself. It forces him, again and again, to face up to those elements in original Christianity which he personally finds obscure or repulsive. He is saved from the temptation to skip or slur or ignore what he finds disagreeable. And the man who yields to that temptation will, of course, never progress in Christian knowledge. For obviously the doctrines which one finds easy are the doctrines which give Christian sanction to truths you already knew. The new truth which you do not know and which you need, must, in the very nature of things, be hidden precisely in the doctrines you least like and least understand. It is just the same here as in science. The phenomenon which is troublesome, which doesn't fit in with the current scientific theories, is the phenomenon which compels reconsideration and thus leads to new knowledge. Science progresses because scientists, instead of running away from such troublesome phenomena or hushing them up, are constantly seeking them out. In the same way, there will be progress in Christian knowledge only as long as we accept the challenge of the difficult or repellent doctrines. A "liberal" Christianity which considers itself free to alter the Faith whenever the Faith looks perplexing or repellent *must* be completely stagnant. Progress is made only into a *resisting* material.

From this there follows a corollary about the Apologist's private reading. There are two questions he will naturally ask himself. (1) Have I been "keeping up", keeping abreast of recent movements in theology? (2) Have I *stood firm* (*super monstratas vias*)[1] amidst all these "winds of doctrine"?[2] I want to say emphatically that the second question is far the more important of the two. Our upbringing and the whole atmosphere of the world we live in make it certain that our main temptation will be that of yielding to winds of doctrine, not that of ignoring them. We are not at all likely to be hidebound: we are very likely indeed to be the slaves of fashion. If one has to choose between reading the new books and reading the old, one must choose the old: not because they are necessarily better but because they contain precisely those truths of which our own age is neglectful. The standard of permanent Christianity must be kept clear in our minds and it is against that standard that we must test all contemporary thought. In fact, we must at all costs *not* move with the times. We serve One who said, "Heaven and Earth shall move with the times, but my words shall not move with the times."[3]

---

[1] The source of this is, I believe, Jeremiah 6:16: "*State super vias et videte, et interrogate de semitis antiquis quae sit via bona, et ambulate in ea*" which is translated "Stand ye in the ways, and see, and ask for the old paths, where is the good way, and walk therein"

[2] Ephesians 4:14

[3] Matthew 24:35; Mark 13:31; Luke 21:33

I am speaking, so far, of theological reading. Scientific reading is a different matter. If you know any science it is very desirable that you should keep it up. We have to answer the current scientific attitude towards Christianity, not the attitude which scientists adopted one hundred years ago. Science is in continual change and we must try to keep abreast of *it*. For the same reason, we must be very cautious of snatching at any scientific theory which, for the moment, seems to be in our favour. We may *mention* such things; but we must mention them lightly and without claiming that they are more than "interesting". Sentences beginning "Science has now proved" should be avoided. If we try to base our apologetic on some recent development in science, we shall usually find that just as we have put the finishing touches to our argument science has changed its mind and quietly withdrawn the theory we have been using as our foundation stone. *Timeo Danaos et dona ferentes*[1] is a sound principle.

While we are on the subject of science, let me digress for a moment. I believe that any Christian who is qualified to write a good popular book on any science may do much more good by that than by any directly apologetic work. The difficulty we are up against is this. We can make people (often) attend to the Christian point of view for half an hour or so; but the moment they have gone away from our lecture or laid down our article, they are plunged back into a world where the opposite position is taken for granted. Every newspaper, film, novel and text book undermines our work. As long as that situation exists, widespread success is simply impossible. We must attack the enemy's line of communication. What we want is not more little books about Christianity, but more little books by Christians on other subjects – with their Christianity

[1] I fear the Greeks even when they bear gifts. Virgil, *Aeneid*, Bk. II, line 49

latent. You can see this most easily if you look at it the other way round. Our Faith is not very likely to be shaken by any book on Hinduism. But if whenever we read an elementary book on Geology, Botany, Politics or Astronomy, we found that its implications were Hindu, that would shake us. It is not the books written in direct defence of Materialism that make the modern man a materialist; it is the materialistic assumptions in all the other books. In the same way, it is not books on Christianity that will really trouble him. But he would be troubled if, whenever he wanted a cheap popular introduction to some science, the best work on the market was always by a Christian. The first step to the reconversion of this country is a series, produced by Christians, which can beat the *Penguins* and the *Thinkers' Library* on their own ground. Its Christianity would have to be latent, not explicit: and *of course* its science perfectly honest. Science *twisted* in the interests of apologetics would be sin and folly. But I must return to my immediate subject.

Our business is to present that which is timeless (the same yesterday, today and tomorrow)[1] in the particular language of our own age. The bad preacher does exactly the opposite: he takes the ideas of our own age and tricks them out in the traditional language of Christianity. Thus, for example, he may think about the Beveridge Report[2] and *talk* about the coming of the Kingdom. The core of his thought is merely contemporary; only the superficies is traditional. But your teaching must be timeless at its heart and wear a modern dress.

This raises the question of Theology and Politics. The nearest I can get to a settlement of the frontier problem

[1] Hebrews 8:8
[2] Sir William H. Beveridge, *Social Insurance and Allied Services*, Command Paper 6404, Parliamentary Session 1942–43 (London: H.M. Stationery Office, 1942). The "Beveridge Report" is a plan for the present Social Security system in Britain

between them is this: that Theology teaches us what ends are desirable and what means are lawful, while Politics teaches what means are effective. Thus Theology tells us that every man ought to have a decent wage. Politics tells by what means this is likely to be attained. Theology tells us which of these means are consistent with justice and charity. On the political question guidance comes not from Revelation but from natural prudence, knowledge of complicated facts and ripe experience. If we have these qualifications we may, of course, state our political opinions: but then we must make it quite clear that we are giving our personal judgement and have no command from the Lord. Not many priests have these qualifications. Most political sermons teach the congregation nothing except what newspapers are taken at the Rectory.

Our great danger at present is lest the Church should continue to practise a merely missionary technique in what has become a missionary situation. A century ago our task was to edify those who had been brought up in the Faith: our present task is chiefly to convert and instruct infidels. Great Britain is as much part of the mission field as China. Now if you were sent to the Bantus you would be taught their language and traditions. You need similar teaching about the language and mental habits of your own uneducated and unbelieving fellow countrymen. Many priests are quite ignorant on this subject. What I know about it I have learned from talking in RAF camps. They were mostly inhabited by Englishmen and, therefore, some of what I shall say may be irrelevant to the situation in Wales. You will sift out what does not apply.

(1) I find that the uneducated Englishman is an almost total sceptic about History. I had expected he would disbelieve the gospels because they contain miracles: but he really disbelieves them because they deal with things

that happened 2,000 years ago. He would disbelieve equally in the battle of Actium if he heard of it. To those who have had our kind of education, his state of mind is very difficult to realize. To us the Present has always appeared as one section in a huge continuous process. In his mind the Present occupies almost the whole field of vision. Beyond it, isolated from it, and quite unimportant, is something called "The Old Days" – a small, comic jungle in which highway men, Queen Elizabeth, knights-in-armour, etc., wander about. Then (strangest of all) beyond The Old Days comes a picture of "Primitive Man". He is "science", not "history", and is therefore felt to be much more real than The Old Days. In other words, the Pre-historic is much more believed in than the Historic.

(2) He has a distrust (very rational in the state of his knowledge) of ancient texts. Thus a man has sometimes said to me, "These records were written in the days before printing, weren't they? and you haven't got the original bit of paper, have you? So what it comes to is that someone wrote something and someone else copied it and someone else copied *that* and so on. Well, by the time it comes to us, it won't be in the least like the original." This is a difficult objection to deal with because one cannot, there and then, start teaching the whole science of textual criticism. But at this point their real religion (i.e. faith in "science") has come to my aid. The assurance that there is a "science" called "Textual Criticism" and that its results (not only as regards the New Testament, but as regards ancient texts in general) are generally accepted, will usually be received without objection. (I need hardly point out that the word "text" must not be used, since to your audience it means only "a scriptural quotation".)

(3) A sense of sin is almost totally lacking. Our situation is thus very different from that of the Apostles. The Pagans

(and still more the *metuentes*[1]) to whom they preached were haunted by a sense of guilt and to them the Gospel was, therefore, "good news". We address people who have been trained to believe that whatever goes wrong in the world is someone else's fault – the Capitalists', the Government's, the Nazis', the Generals', etc. They approach God Himself as His *judges*. They want to know, not whether they can be acquitted for sin, but whether He can be acquitted for creating such a world.

In attacking this fatal insensibility it is useless to direct attention (*a*) to sins your audience do not commit, or (*b*) to things they do, but do not regard as sins. They are usually not drunkards. They are mostly fornicators, but then they do not feel fornication to be wrong. It is, therefore, useless to dwell on either of these subjects. (Now that contraceptives have removed the obviously *uncharitable* element in fornication I do not myself think we can expect people to recognize it as a sin until they have accepted Christianity as a whole.)

I cannot offer you a water-tight technique for awaking the sense of sin. I can only say that, in my experience, if one begins from the sin that has been one's own chief problem during the last week, one is very often surprised at the way this shaft goes home. But whatever method we use, our continual effort must be to get their mind away from public affairs and "crime" and bring them down to brass tacks – to the whole network of spite, greed, envy, unfairness and conceit in the lives of "ordinary decent people" like themselves (and ourselves).

(4) We must learn the language of our audience. And let me say at the outset that it is no use at all laying down *a*

---

[1] The *metuentes* or "god-fearers" were a class of Gentiles who worshipped God without submitting to circumcision and the other ceremonial obligations of the Jewish Law. See Psalm 118:4 and Acts 10:2

priori what the "plain man" does or does not understand. You have to find out by experience. Thus most of us would have supposed that the change from "may truly and indifferently minister justice" to "may truly and impartially"[1] made that place easier to the uneducated; but a priest of my acquaintance discovered that his sexton saw no difficulty in *indifferently* ("It means making no difference between one man and another" he said) but had no idea what *impartially* meant.

On this question of language the best thing I can do is to make a list of words which are used by the people in a sense different from ours.

ATONEMENT. Does not really exist in a spoken modern English, though it would be recognized as "a religious word". In so far as it conveys any meaning to the uneducated I think it means *compensation*. No one word will express to them what Christians mean by *Atonement*: you must paraphrase.

BEING (noun). Never means merely "entity" in popular speech. Often it means what we should call a "personal being" (e.g. a man said to me "I believe in the Holy Ghost but I don't think He is a being").

CATHOLIC means Papistical.

CHARITY. Means (*a*) alms, (*b*) a "charitable organization", (*c*) much more rarely – indulgence (i.e. a "charitable" attitude towards a man is conceived as one that denies or condones his sins, not as one that loves the sinner in spite of them).

CHRISTIAN. Has come to include almost no idea of *belief*. Usually a vague term of approval. The question

---

[1] The first quotation is from prayer for the "Whole state of Christ's Church" in the service of Holy Communion, Prayer Book (1662). The second is the revised form of that same phrase as found in the 1928 Prayer Book

"What do you call a Christian?" has been asked of me again and again. The answer they *wish* to receive is "A Christian is a decent chap who's unselfish, etc.".

CHURCH. Means (*a*) sacred building, (*b*) the clergy. Does *not* suggest to them the "company of all faithful people".[1] Generally used in a bad sense. Direct defence of the Church is part of our duty: but use of the word *Church* where there is no time to defend it alienates sympathy and should be avoided where possible.

CREATIVE. Now means merely "talented", "original". The idea of creation in the theological sense is absent from their minds.

CREATURE means "beast", "irrational animal". Such an expression as "We are only creatures" would almost certainly be misunderstood.

CRUCIFIXION, CROSS, ETC. Centuries of hymnody and religious cant have so exhausted these words that they now very faintly – if at all – convey the idea of execution by torture. It is better to paraphrase; and, for the same reason, to say *flogged* for New Testament *scourged*.[2]

DOGMA. Used by the people only in a bad sense to mean "unproved assertion delivered in an arrogant manner".

IMMACULATE CONCEPTION. In the mouth of an un-educated speaker *always* means *Virgin Birth*.

MORALITY means *chastity*.

PERSONAL. I had argued for at least ten minutes with a man about the existence of a "personal devil" before I discovered that *personal* meant to him *corporeal*. I suspect this of being widespread. When they say they don't believe in a "personal" God they may often mean only that they are not anthropomorphists.

---

[1] A phrase which occurs in the prayer of "Thanksgiving" at the end of the service of Holy Communion in the Book of Common Prayer (1662)
[2] Matthew 27:26; Mark 15:15; John 19:1

POTENTIAL. When used at all is used in an engineering sense: *never* means "possible".

PRIMITIVE. Means crude, clumsy, unfinished, inefficient. "Primitive Christianity" would not mean to them at all what it does to you.

SACRIFICE. Has no associations with temple and altar. They are familiar with this word only in the journalistic sense ("The Nation must be prepared for heavy sacrifices").

SPIRITUAL. Means primarily *immaterial, incorporeal,* but with serious confusions from the Christian uses of πνεῦμα.[1] Hence the idea that whatever is "spiritual" in the sense of "non-sensuous" is somehow *better* than anything sensuous: e.g. they don't really believe that envy could be as bad as drunkenness.

VULGARITY. Usually means obscenity or "smut". There are bad confusions (and not only in uneducated minds) between:

(a) The obscene or lascivious: what is calculated to provoke lust.
(b) The indecorous: what offends against good taste or propriety.
(c) The vulgar proper: what is socially "low".
    "Good" people tend to think (b) as sinful as (a), with the result that others feel (a) to be just as innocent as (b).

To conclude – you must translate every bit of your Theology into the vernacular. This is very troublesome and it means you can say very little in half an hour, but it is essential. It is also of the greatest service to your own thought. I have come to the conviction that if you cannot translate your thoughts into uneducated language, then your thoughts were confused. Power to translate is the test of having really understood one's own meaning. A passage

[1] Which means "spirit", as in 1 Corinthians 14:12

from some theological work for translation into the vernacular ought to be a compulsory paper in every Ordination examination.

I turn now to the question of the actual attack. This may be either emotional or intellectual. If I speak only of the intellectual kind, that is not because I undervalue the other but because, not having been given the gifts necessary for carrying it out, I cannot give advice about it. But I wish to say most emphatically that where a speaker has that gift, the direct evangelical appeal of the "Come to Jesus" type can be as overwhelming today as it was a hundred years ago. I have seen it done, preluded by a religious film and accompanied by hymn singing, and with very remarkable effect. I cannot do it: but those who can ought to do it with all their might. I am not sure that the ideal missionary team ought not to consist of one who argues and one who (in the fullest sense of the word) preaches. Put up your arguer first to undermine their intellectual prejudices; then let the evangelist proper launch his appeal. I have seen this done with great success. But here I must concern myself only with the intellectual attack. *Non omnia possumus omnes*.[1]

And first, a word of encouragement. Uneducated people are not irrational people. I have found that they will endure, and can follow, quite a lot of sustained argument if you go slowly. Often, indeed, the novelty of it (for they have seldom met it before) delights them.

Do not attempt to water Christianity down. There must be no pretence that you can have it with the Supernatural left out. So far as I can see Christianity is precisely the one religion from which the miraculous cannot be separated. You must frankly argue for supernaturalism from the very outset.

The two popular "difficulties" you will probably have to deal with are these.

[1] Not all things can we all do. Virgil, *Eclogues*, Bk. VIII, line 63

(1) "Now that we know how huge the universe is and how insignificant the Earth, it is ridiculous to believe that the universal God should be specially interested in our concerns." In answer to this you must first correct their error about *fact*. The insignificance of Earth in relation to the universe is not a modern discovery: nearly 2,000 years ago Ptolemy (*Almagest*, Bk. I, ch. v) said that in relation to the distance of the fixed stars Earth must be treated as a mathematical point without magnitude. Secondly, you should point out that Christianity says what God has done for Man; it doesn't say (because it doesn't know) what He has or has not done in other parts of the universe. Thirdly, you might recall the parable of the one lost sheep.[1] If Earth has been specially sought by God (which we don't know) that may not imply that it is the most important thing in the universe, but only that it has *strayed*. Finally, challenge the whole tendency to identify size and importance. Is an elephant more important than a man, or a man's leg than his brain?

(2) "People believed in miracles in the Old Days because they didn't then know that they were contrary to the Laws of Nature." But they did. If St Joseph didn't know that a virgin birth was contrary to Nature (i.e. if he didn't yet know the normal origin of babies) why, on discovering his wife's pregnancy, was he "minded to put her away"?[2] Obviously, no event would be recorded as a wonder *unless* the recorders knew the natural order and saw that this was an exception. If people didn't know that the Sun rose in the East they wouldn't be even interested in its once rising in the West. They would not record it as a *miraculum* – nor indeed record it at all. The very idea of "miracle" pre-supposes knowledge of the Laws of Nature; you can't have the idea of an exception until you have the idea of a rule.

[1] Matthew 18:11–14; Luke 15: 4–7
[2] Matthew 1:19

It is very difficult to produce arguments on the popular level for the existence of God. And many of the most popular arguments seem to me invalid. Some of these may be produced in discussion by friendly members of the audience. This raises the whole problem of the "embarrassing supporter". It is brutal (and dangerous) to repel him; it is often dishonest to agree with what he says. I usually try to avoid saying anything about the validity of his argument *in itself* and reply, "Yes. That may do for you and me. But I'm afraid if we take that line our friend here on my left might say, etc., etc."

Fortunately, though very oddly, I have found that people are usually disposed to hear the divinity of Our Lord discussed *before* going into the existence of God. When I began I used, if I were giving two lectures, to devote the first to mere Theism; but I soon gave up this method because it seemed to arouse little interest. The number of clear and determined Atheists is apparently not very large.

When we come to the Incarnation itself, I usually find that some form of the *aut Deus aut malus homo*[1] can be used. The majority of them started with the idea of the "great human teacher" who was deified by His superstitious followers. It must be pointed out how very improbable this is among Jews and how different to anything that happened with Plato, Confucius, Buddha, Muhammad. The Lord's own words and claims (of which many are quite ignorant) must be forced home. (The whole case, on a popular level, is very well put indeed in Chesterton's *The Everlasting Man*.)

Something will usually have to be said about the historicity of the gospels. You who are trained theologians will be able to do this in ways which I could not. My own line was to say that I was a professional literary critic and I thought I did know the difference between legend and

[1] Either God or a bad man

historical writing: that the gospels were certainly not legends (in one sense they're not *good* enough): and that if they are not history then they are realistic prose fiction of a kind which actually never existed before the eighteenth century. Little episodes such as Jesus writing in the dust when they brought Him the woman taken in adultery[1] (which have no *doctrinal* significance at all) are the mark.

One of the great difficulties is to keep before the audience's mind the question of Truth. They always think you are recommending Christianity not because it is *true* but because it is *good*. And in the discussion they will at every moment try to escape from the issue "True — or False" into stuff about a good society, or morals, or the incomes of Bishops, or the Spanish Inquisition, or France, or Poland — or anything whatever. You have to keep forcing them back, and again back, to the real point. Only thus will you be able to undermine (*a*) Their belief that a certain amount of "religion" is desirable but one mustn't carry it too far. One must keep on pointing out that Christianity is a statement which, if false, is of *no* importance, and, if true, of infinite importance. The one thing it cannot be is moderately important. (*b*) Their firm belief of Article XVIII.[2] Of course it should be pointed out that, though all salvation is through Jesus, we need not conclude that He cannot save those who have not explicitly accepted Him in this life. And it should (at least in my judgement) be made clear that we are not pronouncing all other religions to be totally false, but rather saying that in Christ whatever is true in all religions is consummated and perfected. But, on

[1] John 8:3–8
[2] Article XVIII in the Prayer Book: Of *obtaining eternal Salvation only by the Name of Christ*, which says "They also are to be had accursed that presume to say, That every man shall be saved by the Law or Sect which he professeth, so that he be diligent to frame his life according to that Law, and the light of Nature. For holy Scripture doth set out unto us only the Name of Jesus Christ, whereby men must be saved."

the other hand, I think we must attack wherever we meet it the nonsensical idea that mutually exclusive propositions about God can both be true.

For my own part, I have sometimes told my audience that the only two things really worth considering are Christianity and Hinduism. (Islam is only the greatest of the Christian heresies, Buddhism only the greatest of the Hindu heresies. Real Paganism is dead. All that was best in Judaism and Platonism survives in Christianity.) There isn't really, for an adult mind, this infinite variety of religions to consider. We may *salva reverentia*[1] divide religions, as we do soups, into "thick" and "clear". By Thick I mean those which have orgies and ecstasies and mysteries and local attachments: Africa is full of Thick religions. By Clear I mean those which are philosophical, ethical and universalizing: Stoicism, Buddhism and the Ethical Church are Clear religions. Now if there is a true religion it must be both Thick and Clear: for the true God must have made both the child and the man, both the savage and the citizen, both the head and the belly. And the only two religions that fulfil this condition are Hinduism and Christianity. But Hinduism fulfils it imperfectly. The Clear religion of the Brahmin hermit in the jungle and the Thick religion of the neighbouring temple go on *side by side*. The Brahmin hermit doesn't bother about the temple prostitution, nor the worshipper in the temple about the hermit's metaphysic. But Christianity really breaks down the middle wall of the partition. It takes a convert from central Africa and tells him to obey an enlightened universalist ethic: it takes a twentieth-century academic prig like me and tells me to go fasting to a Mystery, to drink the blood of the Lord. The savage convert has to be Clear: I have to be Thick. That is how one knows one has come to the real religion.

[1] Without outraging reverence

One last word. I have found that nothing is more dangerous to one's own faith than the work of an apologist. No doctrine of that Faith seems to me so spectral, so unreal as one that I have just successfully defended in a public debate. For a moment, you see, it has seemed to rest on oneself: as a result, when you go away from that debate, it seems no stronger than that weak pillar. That is why we apologists take our lives in our hands and can be saved only by falling back continually from the web of our own arguments, as from our intellectual counters, into the Reality – from Christian apologetics into Christ Himself. That also is why we need one another's continual help – *oremus pro invicem*.[1]

[1] Let us pray for each other

2

Answers to Questions on Christianity[1]

(1944)

Lewis: I have been asked to open with a few words on Christianity and Modern Industry. Now Modern Industry is a subject of which I know nothing at all. But for that very reason it may illustrate what Christianity, in my opinion, does and does not do. Christianity does *not* replace the technical. When it tells you to feed the hungry it doesn't give you lessons in cookery. If you want to learn *that*, you must go to a cook rather than a Christian. If you are not a professional economist and have no experience of industry, simply being a Christian won't give you the answer to industrial problems. My own idea is that modern industry is a radically hopeless system. You can improve wages, hours, conditions, etc., but all that doesn't cure the deepest trouble: i.e. that numbers of people are kept all their lives doing dull repetition work which gives no full play to their faculties. How that is to be overcome, I do not know. If a single country abandoned the system it would merely fall a prey to the other countries which hadn't abandoned it. I don't know the solution: that is not the kind of thing Christianity teaches a person like me. Let's now carry on with the questions:

[1] The answers to questions printed here were given by Lewis at a "One Man Brains Trust" held on 18th April 1944 at the Head Office of Electric and Musical Industries Ltd, Hayes, Middlesex. Shorthand notes were made and a typescript was sent to Lewis. He revised it a little, and it was printed as a booklet. Mr H.W. Bowen was the question master

Question 1
Christians are taught to love their neighbours. How, therefore, can they justify their attitude of supporting the war?

Lewis: You are told to love your neighbour as yourself. How do you love yourself? When I look into my own mind, I find that I do not love myself by thinking myself a dear old chap or having affectionate feelings. I do not think that I love myself because I am particularly good, but just because I am myself and quite apart from my character. I might detest something which I have done. Nevertheless, I do not cease to love myself. In other words, that definite distinction that Christians make between hating sin and loving the sinner is one that you have been making in your own case since you were born. You dislike what you have done, but you don't cease to love yourself. You may even think that you ought to be hanged. You may even think that you ought to go to the police and own up and be hanged. Love is not affectionate feeling, but a steady wish for the loved person's ultimate good as far as it can be obtained. It seems to me, therefore, that when the worst comes to the worst, if you cannot restrain a man by any method except by trying to kill him, then a Christian must do that. That is my answer. But I may be wrong. It is very difficult to answer, of course.

Question 2
Supposing a factory worker asked you: "How can I find God?" How would you reply?

Lewis: I don't see how the problem would be different for a factory worker than for anyone else. The primary thing about any man is that he is a human being, sharing all the ordinary human temptations and assets. What is the special problem about the factory worker? But perhaps it is worth saying this:

Christianity really does two things about conditions here and now in this world:

(1) It tries to make them as good as possible, i.e. to reform them; but also

(2) It fortifies you against them in so far as they remain bad.

If what was in the questioner's mind was this problem of repetition work, then the factory worker's difficulty is the same as any other man confronted with any sorrow or difficulty. People will find God if they consciously seek from Him the right attitude towards all unpleasant things ... if that is the point of the question?

Question 3
Will you please say how you would define a practising Christian. Are there any other varieties?

Lewis: Certainly there are a great many other varieties. It depends, of course, on what you mean by "practising Christian". If you mean one who has practised Christianity in every respect at every moment of his life, then there is only One on record – Christ Himself. In that sense there are no practising Christians, but only Christians who, in varying degrees, try to practise it and fail in varying degrees and then start again. A perfect practice of Christianity would, of course, consist in a perfect imitation of the life of Christ – I mean, in so far as it was applicable in one's own particular circumstances. Not in an idiotic sense – it doesn't mean that every Christian should grow a beard, or be a bachelor, or become a travelling preacher. It means that every single act and feeling, every experience, whether pleasant or unpleasant, must be referred to God. It means looking at everything as something that comes from Him, and always looking to Him and asking His will first, and saying: "How would He wish me to deal with this?"

A kind of picture or pattern (in a very remote way) of the relation between the perfect Christian and his God, would be the relation of the good dog to its master. This is only a very imperfect picture, though, because the dog hasn't reason like its master: whereas we do share in God's reason, even if in an imperfect and interrupted way ("interrupted" because we don't think rationally for very long at a time – it's too tiring – and we haven't information to understand things fully, and our intelligence itself has certain limitations). In that way we are more like God than the dog is like us, though, of course, there are other ways in which the dog is more like us than we are like God. It is only an illustration.

Question 4
What justification on ethical grounds and on the grounds of social expediency exists for the Church's attitude towards Venereal Disease and prophylaxis and publicity in connection with it?

Lewis: I need further advice on that question, and then perhaps I can answer it. Can the questioner say which Church he has in mind?
Voice: The Church concerned is the Church of England, and its attitude, though not written, is implicit in that it has more or less banned all publicity in connection with prophylactic methods of combating Venereal Disease. The view of some is that moral punishment should not be avoided.
Lewis: I haven't myself met any clergymen of the Church of England who held that view: and I don't hold it myself. There are obvious objections to it. After all, it isn't only Venereal Disease that can be regarded as a punishment for

bad conduct. Indigestion in old age may be the result of overeating in earlier life: but no one objects to advertisements for Beecham's Pills. I, at any rate, strongly dissent from the view you've mentioned.

Question 5

Many people feel resentful or unhappy because they think they are the target of unjust fate. These feelings are stimulated by bereavement, illness, deranged domestic or working conditions, or the observation of suffering in others. What is the Christian view of this problem?

Lewis: The Christian view is that men are created to be in a certain relationship to God (if we are in that relation to Him, the right relation to one another will follow inevitably). Christ said it was difficult for "the rich" to enter the Kingdom of Heaven,[1] referring, no doubt, to "riches" in the ordinary sense. But I think it really covers riches in every sense – good fortune, health, popularity, and all the things one wants to have. All these things tend – just as money tends – to make you feel independent of God, because if you have them you are happy already and contented in this life. You don't want to turn away to anything more, and so you try to rest in a shadowy happiness as if it could last for ever. But God wants to give you a real and eternal happiness. Consequently He may have to take all these "riches" away from you: if He doesn't, you will go on relying on them. It sounds cruel, doesn't it? But I am beginning to find out that what people call the cruel doctrines are really the kindest ones in the long run. I used to think it was a "cruel" doctrine to say that troubles and sorrows were "punishments". But I find in practice that when you are in trouble, the moment you regard it as a "punishment", it becomes easier to bear. If you think of

[1] Matthew 19:23; Mark 10:23; Luke 18:24

this world as a place intended simply for our happiness, you find it quite intolerable: think of it as a place of training and correction and it's not so bad.

Imagine a set of people all living in the same building. Half of them think it is a hotel, the other half think it is a prison. Those who think it a hotel might regard it as quite intolerable, and those who thought it was a prison might decide that it was really surprisingly comfortable. So that what seems the ugly doctrine is one that comforts and strengthens you in the end. The people who try to hold an optimistic view of this world would become pessimists: the people who hold a pretty stern view of it become optimistic.

Question 6

Materialists and some astronomers suggest that the solar planetary system and life as we know it was brought about by an accidental stellar collision. What is the Christian view of this theory?

Lewis: If the solar system was brought about by an accidental collision, then the appearance of organic life on this planet was also an accident, and the whole evolution of Man was an accident too. If so, then all our present thoughts are mere accidents – the accidental by-product of the movement of atoms. And this holds for the thoughts of the materialists and astronomers as well as for anyone else's. But if *their* thoughts – i.e. of materialism and astronomy – are merely accidental by-products, why should we believe them to be true? I see no reason for believing that one accident should be able to give me a correct account of all the other accidents. It's like expecting that the accidental shape taken by the splash when you upset a milk jug should give you a correct account of how the jug was made and why it was upset.

Question 7
Is it true that Christianity (especially the Protestant forms) tends to produce a gloomy, joyless condition of society which is like a pain in the neck to most people?

Lewis: As to the distinction between Protestant and other forms of Christianity, it is very difficult to answer. I find by reading about the sixteenth century, that people like Sir Thomas More, for whom I have a great respect, always regarded Martin Luther's doctrines not as gloomy thinking, but as wishful thinking. I doubt whether we can make a distinction between Protestant and other forms in this respect. Whether Protestantism is gloomy and whether Christianity at all produces gloominess, I find it very difficult to answer, as I have never lived in a completely non-Christian society nor a completely Christian one, and I wasn't there in the sixteenth century, and only have my knowledge from reading books. I think there is about the same amount of fun and gloom in all periods. The poems, novels, letters, etc., of every period all seem to show that. But again, I don't really know the answer, of course. I wasn't there.

Question 8
Is it true that Christians must be prepared to live a life of personal discomfort and self-sacrifice in order to qualify for "Pie in the Sky"?

Lewis: All people, whether Christians or not, must be prepared to live a life of discomfort. It is impossible to accept Christianity for the sake of finding comfort: but the Christian tries to lay himself open to the will of God, to do what God wants him to do. You don't know in advance whether God is going to set you to do something difficult or painful, or something that you will quite like; and some people of heroic mould are disappointed when the job doled out to them turns out to be something quite nice. But you must be prepared for the unpleasant things and the discomforts. I don't mean fasting, and things like that. They are a different matter. When you are training soldiers in manoeuvres, you practise with blank ammunition because you would like them to have practice before meeting the real enemy. So we must practise in abstaining from pleasures which are not in themselves wicked. If you don't abstain from pleasure, you won't be good when the time comes along. It is purely a matter of practice.

Voice: Are not practices like fasting and self-denial borrowed from earlier or more primitive religions?

Lewis: I can't say for certain which bits came into Christianity from earlier religions. An enormous amount did. I should find it hard to believe Christianity if that were not so. I couldn't believe that nine hundred and ninety-nine religions were completely false and the remaining one true. In reality, Christianity is primarily the fulfilment of the Jewish religion, but also the fulfilment of what was vaguely hinted in all the religions at their best. What was vaguely seen in them all comes into focus in Christianity – just as God Himself comes into focus by becoming a Man. I take it that the speaker's remarks on earlier religions are based on evidence about modern savages. I don't think it is good evidence. Modern savages usually represent some decay in culture – you find them doing things which look as if they had a fairly civilized basis once, which they have forgotten. To assume that primitive man was exactly like the modern savage is unsound.

Voice: Could you say any more on how one discovers whether a task is laid on one by God, or whether it comes in some other way? If we cannot distinguish between the pleasant and the unpleasant things, it is a complicated matter.

Lewis: We are guided by the ordinary rules of moral behaviour, which I think are more or less common to the human race and quite reasonable and demanded by the circumstances. I don't mean anything like sitting down and waiting for a supernatural vision.

Voice: We don't qualify for heaven by practice, but salvation is obtained at the Cross. We do nothing to obtain it, but follow Christ. We may have pain or tribulation, but nothing we do qualifies us for heaven, but Christ.

Lewis: The controversy about faith and works is one that has gone on for a very long time, and it is a highly technical matter. I personally rely on the paradoxical text: "Work out your own salvation . . . for it is God that worketh in you."[1] It looks as if in one sense we do nothing, and in another case we do a damned lot. "Work out your own salvation with fear and trembling,"[2] but you must have it in you before you can work it out. But I have no wish to go further into it, as it would interest no one but the Christians present, would it?

Question 9

Would the application of Christian standards bring to an end or greatly reduce scientific and material progress? In other words, is it wrong for a Christian to be ambitious and strive for personal success?

Lewis: It is easier to think of a simplified example. How would the application of Christianity affect anyone on a desert island? Would he be less likely to build a comfortable hut? The answer is "No". There might come a particular moment, of course, when Christianity would tell him to bother less about the hut, i.e. if he were in danger of coming to think that the hut was the most important thing

[1] Philippians 2: 12–13
[2] ibid.

in the universe. But there is no evidence that Christianity would prevent him from building it.

Ambition! We must be careful what we mean by it. If it means the desire to get ahead of other people – which is what I think it does mean – then it is bad. If it means simply wanting to do a thing well, then it is good. It isn't wrong for an actor to want to act his part as well as it can possibly be acted, but the wish to have his name in bigger type than the other actors is a bad one.

Voice: It's all right to be a General, but if it is one's ambition to be a General, then you shouldn't become one.

Lewis: The mere event of becoming a General isn't either right or wrong in itself. What matters morally is your attitude towards it. The man may be thinking about winning a war; he may be wanting to be a General because he honestly thinks that he has a good plan and is glad of a chance to carry it out. That's all right. But if he is thinking: "What can I get out of the job?" or "How can I get on the front page of the *Illustrated News*?" then it is all wrong. And what we call "ambition" usually means the wish to be more conspicuous or more successful than someone else. It is this competitive element in it that is bad. It is perfectly reasonable to want to dance well or to look nice. But when the dominant wish is to dance better or look nicer than the others – when you begin to feel that if the others danced as well as you or looked as nice as you, that would take all the fun out of it – then you are going wrong.

Voice: I am wondering how far we can ascribe to the work of the Devil those very legitimate desires that we indulge in. Some people have a very sensitive conception of the presence of the Devil. Others haven't. Is the Devil as real as we think he is? That doesn't trouble some people, since they have no desire to be good, but others are continually harassed by the Old Man himself.

Lewis: No reference to the Devil or devils is included in any Christian Creeds, and it is quite possible to be a Christian without believing in them. I do believe such beings exist, but that is my own affair. Supposing there to be such beings, the degree to which humans were conscious of their presence would presumably vary very much. I mean, the more a man was in the Devil's power, the less he would be aware of it, on the principle that a man is still fairly sober as long as he knows he's drunk. It is the people who are fully awake and trying hard to be good who would be most aware of the Devil. It is when you start arming against Hitler that you first realize your country is full of Nazi agents. Of course, they don't want you to know they are there. In the same way, the Devil doesn't want you to believe in the Devil. If devils exist, their first aim is to give you an anaesthetic – to put you off your guard. Only if that fails, do you become aware of them.

Voice: Does Christianity retard scientific advancement? Or does it approve of those who help spiritually others who are on the road to perdition, by scientifically removing the environmental causes of the trouble?

Lewis: Yes. In the abstract it is certainly so. At a particular moment, if most human beings are concentrating only on material improvements in the environment, it may be the duty of Christians to point out (and pretty loudly) that this isn't the only thing that matters. But as a general rule it is in favour of all knowledge and all that will help the human race in any way.

Question 10

The Bible was written thousands of years ago for people in a lower state of mental development than today. Many portions seem preposterous in the light of modern knowledge. In view of this, should not the Bible be rewritten with the object of discarding the fabulous and re-interpreting the remainder?

Lewis: First of all as to the people in a lower state of mental development. I am not so sure what lurks behind that. If it means that people ten thousand years ago did not know a good many things that we know now, of course, I agree. But if it means that there has been any advance in *intelligence* in that time, I believe there is no evidence for any such thing. The Bible can be divided into two parts – the Old and the New Testaments. The Old Testament contains fabulous elements. The New Testament consists mostly of teaching, not of narrative at all: but where it *is* narrative, it is, in my opinion, historical. As to the fabulous element in the Old Testament, I very much doubt if you would be wise to chuck it out. What you get is something *coming gradually into focus*. First you get, scattered through the heathen religions all over the world – but still quite vague and mythical – the idea of a god who is killed and broken and then comes to life again. No one knows where he is supposed to have lived and died; he's not historical. Then you get the Old Testament. Religious ideas get a bit more focused. Everything is now connected with a particular nation. And it comes still more into focus as it goes on. Jonah and the Whale,[1] Noah and his Ark,[2] are fabulous; but the court history of King David[3] is probably as reliable as the court history of Louis XIV. Then, in the New Testament the *thing really happens*. The dying god really appears – as a historical Person, living in a definite place and time. If we *could* sort out all the fabulous elements in the earlier stages and separate them from the historical ones, I think we might lose an essential part of the whole process. That is my own idea.

[1] The Book of Jonah
[2] Genesis 6–8
[3] 2 Samuel 2–1 Kings 2

Question 11
Which of the religions of the world gives to its followers the greatest happiness?

Lewis: Which of the religions of the world gives to its followers the greatest happiness? While it lasts, the religion of worshipping oneself is the best.

I have an elderly acquaintance of about eighty, who has lived a life of unbroken selfishness and self-admiration from the earliest years, and is, more or less, I regret to say, one of the happiest men I know. From the moral point of view it is very difficult! I am not approaching the question from that angle. As you perhaps know, I haven't always been a Christian. I didn't go to religion to make me happy. I always knew a bottle of port would do that. If you want a religion to make you feel really comfortable, I certainly don't recommend Christianity. I am certain there must be a patent American article on the market which will suit you far better, but I can't give any advice on it.

Question 12
Are there any unmistakable outward signs in a person surrendered to God? Would he be cantankerous? Would he smoke?

Lewis: I think of the advertisements for "White Smiles" Tooth Paste, saying that it is the best on the market. If they are true, it would follow that:

(1) Anyone who starts using it will have better teeth.
(2) Anyone using it has better teeth than he would have if he weren't using it.

But you can't test it in the case of one who has naturally bad teeth and uses it, and compare him with a healthy Negro who has never used toothpaste at all.

Take the case of a sour old maid, who is a Christian, but cantankerous. On the other hand, take some pleasant and popular fellow, but who has never been to church. Who knows how much more cantankerous the old maid might be if she were *not* a Christian, and how much more likeable the nice fellow might be if he *were* a Christian? You can't judge Christianity simply by comparing the *product* in those two people; you would need to know what kind of raw material Christ was working on in both cases.

As an illustration, let us take a case of industrialism. Let us take two factories:

Factory A with poor and inadequate plant, and
Factory B with first-class modern plant.

You can't judge by the outside. You must consider the plant and methods by which they are run, and considering the plant at Factory A, it may be a wonder it does anything at all; and considering the new machinery at Factory B, it may be a wonder it doesn't do better.

Question 13
What is your opinion about raffles within the plant – no matter how good the cause – which, not infrequently, is given less prominence than the alluring list of prizes?

Lewis: Gambling ought never to be an important part of a man's life. If it is a way in which large sums of money are transferred from person to person without doing any good (e.g. producing employment, good will, etc.) then it is a bad thing. If it is carried out on a small scale, I am not sure that it is bad. I don't know much about it, because it is about the only vice to which I have no temptation at all, and I think it is a risk to talk about things which are not in my own make-up, because I don't understand them. If anyone comes to me asking me to play bridge for money, I just say: "How much do you hope to win? Take it and go away."

Question 14
Many people are quite unable to understand the theological differences which have caused divisions in the Christian Church. Do you consider that these differences are fundamental, and is the time now ripe for re-union?

Lewis: The time is always ripe for re-union. Divisions between Christians are a sin and a scandal, and Christians ought at all times to be making contributions towards re-union, if it is only by their prayers. I am only a layman and a recent Christian, and I do not know much about these things, but in all the things which I have written and thought I have always stuck to traditional, dogmatic positions. The result is that letters of agreement reach me from what are ordinarily regarded as the most different kinds of Christians; for instance, I get letters from Jesuits, monks, nuns, and also from Quakers and Welsh Dissenters, and so on. So it seems to me that the "extreme" elements in every Church are nearest one another, and the liberal and "broad-minded" people in each Body could never be united at all. The world of dogmatic Christianity is a place in which thousands of people of quite different types keep on saying the same thing, and the world of "broad-mindedness" and watered-down "religion" is a world where a small number of people (all of the same type) say totally different things and change their minds every few minutes. We shall never get re-union from them.

Question 15
In the past the Church used various kinds of compulsion in attempts to force a particular brand of Christianity on the community. Given sufficient power, is there not a danger of this sort of thing happening again?

Lewis: Yes. I hear nasty rumours coming from Spain. Persecution is a temptation to which all men are exposed. I had a postcard signed "M.D." saying that anyone who expressed and published his belief in the Virgin Birth should be stripped and flogged. That shows you how easily persecution of Christians by the non-Christians might come back. Of course, they wouldn't call it persecution: they'd call it "Compulsory re-education of the ideologically unfit", or something like that. But, of course, I have to admit that Christians themselves have been persecutors in the past. It was worse of them, because *they* ought to have known better: they weren't worse in any other way. I detest every kind of religious compulsion: only the other day I was writing an angry letter to *The Spectator* about Church Parades in the Home Guard!

Question 16

Is attendance at a place of worship or membership with a Christian community necessary to a Christian way of life?

Lewis: That's a question which I cannot answer. My own experience is that when I first became a Christian, about fourteen years ago, I thought that I could do it on my own, by retiring to my rooms and reading theology, and I wouldn't go to the churches and gospel halls; and then later I found that it was the only way of flying your flag; and, of course, I found that this meant being a target. It is extraordinary how inconvenient to your family it becomes for you to get up early to go to church. It doesn't matter so much if you get up early for anything else, but if you get up early to go to church it's very selfish of you and you upset the house. If there is anything in the teaching of the New Testament which is in the nature of a command, it is that you are obliged to take the Sacrament,[1] and you can't do it

---

[1] John 6: 53–54: "Except ye eat the flesh of the Son of man, and drink his blood, ye have no life in you. Whoso eateth my flesh, and drinketh my blood, hath eternal life; and I will raise him up at the last day."

without going to church. I disliked very much their hymns, which I considered to be fifth-rate poems set to sixth-rate music. But as I went on I saw the great merit of it. I came up against different people of quite different outlooks and different education, and then gradually my conceit just began peeling off. I realized that the hymns (which were just sixth-rate music) were, nevertheless, being sung with devotion and benefit by an old saint in elastic-sided boots in the opposite pew, and then you realize that you aren't fit to clean those boots. It gets you out of your solitary conceit. It is not for me to lay down laws, as I am only a layman, and I don't know much.

Question 17
If it is true that one has only to want God enough in order to find Him, how can I make myself want Him enough to enable myself to find Him?

Lewis: If you don't want God, why are you so anxious to want to want Him? I think that in reality the want is a real one, and I should say that this person has in fact found God, although it may not be fully recognized yet. We are not always aware of things at the time they happen. At any rate, what is more important is that God has found this person, and that is the main thing.

3

Why I Am Not a Pacifist

The question is whether to serve in the wars at the command of the civil society to which we belong is a wicked action, or an action morally indifferent, or an action morally obligatory. In asking how to decide this question, we are raising a much more general question: how do we decide what is good or evil? The usual answer is that we decide by conscience. But probably no one thinks now of conscience as a separate faculty, like one of the senses. Indeed, it cannot be so thought of. For an autonomous faculty like a sense cannot be argued with; you cannot argue a man into seeing green if he sees blue. But the conscience can be altered by argument; and if you did not think so, you would not have asked me to come and argue with you about the morality of obeying the civil law when it tells us to serve in the wars. Conscience, then, means the whole man engaged in a particular subject matter.

But even in this sense conscience still has two meanings. It can mean (a) the pressure a man feels upon his will to do what he thinks is right; (b) his judgement as to what the content of right and wrong are. In sense (a) conscience is always to be followed. It is the sovereign of the universe, which "if it had power as it has right, would absolutely rule the world". It is not to be argued with, but obeyed, and even to question it is to incur guilt. But in sense (b) it is a very different matter. People may be mistaken about wrong and right; most people in some degree are mistaken. By what means are mistakes in this field to be corrected?

The most useful analogy here is that of Reason — by which I do not mean some separate faculty but, once more, the whole man judging, only judging this time not about good and evil, but about truth and falsehood. Now any concrete train of reasoning involves three elements.

Firstly, there is the reception of facts to reason about. These facts are received either from our own senses, or from the report of other minds; that is, either experience or authority supplies us with our material. But each man's experience is so limited that the second source is the more usual; of every hundred facts upon which to reason, ninety-nine depend on authority.

Secondly, there is the direct, simple act of the mind perceiving self-evident truth, as when we see that if A and B both equal C, then they equal each other. This act I call intuition.

Thirdly, there is an art or skill of arranging the facts so as to yield a series of such intuitions which linked together produce a proof of the truth or falsehood of the proposition we are considering. Thus in a geometrical proof each step is seen by intuition, and to fail to see it is to be not a bad geometrician but an idiot. The skill comes in arranging the material into a series of intuitable "steps". Failure to do this does not mean idiocy, but only lack of ingenuity or invention. Failure to follow it need not mean idiocy, but either inattention or a defect of memory which forbids us to hold all the intuitions together.

Now all correction of errors in reasoning is really correction of the first or the third element. The second, the intuitional element, cannot be corrected if it is wrong, nor supplied if it is lacking. You can give the man new facts. You can invent a simpler proof, that is, a simpler con-catenation of intuitable truths. But when you come to an absolute inability to see any one of the self-evident steps out of which the proof is built, then you can do nothing. No doubt this absolute inability is much rarer than we suppose. Every teacher knows that people are constantly protesting that they "can't see" some self-evident inference, but the supposed inability is usually a refusal to see, resulting either from some passion which *wants* not to see the truth in question or else from sloth which does not want to think at all. But when the inability is real, argument is at an end. You cannot produce rational intuition by argument, because argument depends upon rational intuition. Proof rests upon the unprovable which has to be just "seen". Hence faulty intuition is incorrigible. It does not follow that it cannot be trained by practice in attention and in the mortification of disturbing passions, or corrupted by the opposite habits. But it is not amenable to correction by argument.

Before leaving the subject of Reason, I must point out that authority not only combines with experience to produce the raw material, the "facts", but also has to be frequently used instead of reasoning itself as a method of getting conclusions. For example, few of us have followed the reasoning on which even ten percent of the truths we believe are based. We accept them on authority from the experts and are wise to do so, for though we are thereby sometimes deceived, yet we should have to live like savages if we did not.

Now all three elements are found also in conscience. The facts, as before, come from experience and authority. I do not mean "moral facts" but those facts about actions without holding which we could not raise moral questions at all — for we should not even be discussing Pacifism if we did not know what war and killing meant, nor Chastity, if we had not yet learned what schoolmasters used to call "the facts of life". Secondly, there are the pure intuitions of utterly simple good and evil as such. Third, there is the process of argument by which you arrange the intuitions so as to convince a man that a particular act is wrong or right. And finally, there is authority as a substitute for argument, telling a man of some wrong or right which he would not otherwise have discovered, and rightly accepted if the man has good reason to believe the authority wiser and better than himself. The main difference between Reason and Conscience is an alarming one. It is thus: that while the unarguable intuitions on which all depend are liable to be corrupted by passion when we are considering truth and falsehood, they are much more liable, they are almost certain to be corrupted when we are considering good and evil. For then we are concerned with some action to be here and now done or left undone by ourselves. And we should not be considering that action at all unless we had some wish either to do or not to do it, so that in this sphere we are bribed from the very beginning. Hence the value of authority in checking, or even superseding, our own activity is much greater in this sphere than in that of Reason. Hence, too, human beings must be trained in obedience to the moral intuitions almost before they have them, and years before they are rational enough to discuss them, or they will be corrupted before the time for discussion arrives.

These basic moral intuitions are the only element in Conscience which cannot be argued about; if there can be a difference of opinion which does not reveal one of the parties as a moral idiot, then it is not an intuition. They are the ultimate preferences of the will for love rather than hatred, and happiness rather than misery. There are people so corrupted as to have lost even these, just as there are people who can't see the simplest proof, but in the main these can be said to be the voice of humanity as such. And they are unarguable. But here the trouble begins. People are constantly claiming this unarguable and unanswerable status for moral judgements which are not really intuitions at all but remote consequences or particular applications of them, eminently open to discussion since the consequences may be illogically drawn or the application falsely made.

51

Thus you may meet a "temperance" fanatic who claims to have an unanswerable intuition that all strong drink is forbidden. Really he can have nothing of the sort. The real intuition is that health and harmony are good. Then there is a generalization from facts to the effect that drunkenness produces disease and quarrelling, and perhaps also, if the fanatic is Christian, the voice of Authority saying that the body is the temple of the Holy Ghost. Then there is a conclusion that what can always be abused had better never be used at all – a conclusion eminently suited for discussion. Finally, there is the process whereby early associations, arrogance, and the like turn the remote conclusion into something which the man thinks unarguable because he does not wish to argue about it.

This, then is our first canon for moral decisions. Conscience in the (a) sense, the thing that moves us to do right, has absolute authority, but conscience in the (b) sense, our judgement as to what is right, is a mixture of inarguable intuitions and highly arguable processes of reasoning or of submission to authority; and nothing is to be treated as an intuition unless it is such that no good man has ever dreamed of doubting. The man who "just feels" that total abstinence from drink or marriage is obligatory is to be treated like the man who "just feels sure" that *Henry VIII* is not by Shakespeare, or that vaccination does no good. For a mere unargued conviction is in place only when we are dealing with the axiomatic; and these views are not axiomatic.

I therefore begin by ruling out one Pacifist position which probably no one present holds, but which conceivably might be held – that of the man who claims to know on the ground of immediate intuition that all killing of human beings is in all circumstances an absolute evil. With the man who reaches the same result by reasoning or authority, I can argue. Of the man who claims not to reach it but to start there, we can only say that he can have no such intuition as he claims. He is mistaking an opinion, or, more likely, a passion, for an intuition. Of course, it would be rude to say this to him. *To* him we can only say that if he is not a moral idiot, then unfortunately the rest of the human race, including its best and wisest, are, and that argument across such a chasm is impossible.

Having ruled out this extreme case, I return to enquire how we are to decide on a question of morals. We have seen that every moral judgement involves facts, intuition and reasoning, and, if we are wise enough to be humble, it will involve some regard for authority as well. Its strength depends on the strength of these four factors. Thus if I find that the facts on which I am working are clear and little disputed, that the basic intuition is unmistakably an intuition, that the reasoning which connects this intuition with the particular judgement is strong, and that I am in agreement or (at worst) not in disagreement with authority, then I can trust my moral judgement with reasonable confidence. And if, in addition, I find little reason to suppose that any passion has secretly swayed my mind, this confidence is confirmed. If, on the other hand, I find the facts doubtful, the supposed intuition by no means obvious to all good men, the reasoning weak, and authority against me, then I ought to conclude that I am probably wrong. And if the conclusion which I have reached turns out also to flatter some strong passion of my own, then my suspicion should deepen into moral certainty. By "moral certainty" I mean that degree of certainty proper to moral decisions; for mathematical certainty is not here to be looked for. I now apply these tests to the judgement, "It is immoral to obey when the civil society of which I am a member commands me to serve in the wars!"

First as to the facts. The main relevant fact admitted by all parties is that war is very disagreeable. The main contention urged as fact by pacifists would be that wars always do more harm than good. How is one to find out whether this is true? It belongs to a class of historical generalizations which involve a comparison between the actual consequences of some actual event and a consequence which might have followed if that event had not occurred. "Wars do no good" involves the proposition that if the Greeks had yielded to Xerxes and the Romans to Hannibal, the course of history ever since would have been perhaps better, but certainly no worse than it actually has been; that a Mediterranean world in which Carthaginian power succeeded Persian would have been at least as good and happy and as fruitful for all posterity as the actual Mediterranean world in which Roman power succeeded Greek. My point is not that such an opinion seems to me overwhelmingly improbable. My point is that both opinions are merely speculative; there is no conceivable way of convincing a man of either. Indeed it is doubtful whether the whole conception of "what would have happened" – that is, of unrealized possibilities – is more than an imaginative technique for giving a vivid rhetorical account of what did happen.

That wars do no good is then so far from being a fact that it hardly ranks as a historical opinion. Nor is the matter mended by saying "modern wars"; how are we to decide whether the total effect would have been better or worse if Europe had submitted to Germany in 1914? It is, of course, true that wars never do half the good which the leaders of the belligerents say they are going to do. Nothing ever does half the good – perhaps nothing ever does half the evil – which is expected of it. And that may be a sound argument for not pitching one's propaganda too high. But it is no argument against war. If a Germanized Europe in 1914 would have been an evil, then the war which prevented that evil was, so far, justified. To call it useless because it did not also cure slums and unemployment is like coming up to a man who has just succeeded in defending himself from a man-eating tiger and saying, "It's no good, old chap. This hasn't really cured your rheumatism!"

On the test of the fact, then, I find the Pacifist position weak. It seems to me that history is full of useful wars as well as of useless wars. If all that can be brought against the frequent appearance of utility is mere speculation about what could have happened, I am not converted.

I turn next to the intuition. There is no question of discussion once we have found it; there is only the danger of mistaking for an intuition something which is really a conclusion and therefore needs argument. We want something which no good man has ever disputed; we are in search of platitude. The relevant intuition seems to be that love is good and hatred bad, or that helping is good and harming bad.

We have next to consider whether reasoning leads us from this intuition to the Pacifist conclusion or not. And the first thing I notice is that intuition can lead to no action until it is limited in some way or other. You cannot do *simply* good to *simply* Man; you must do this or that good to this or that man. And if you do *this* good, you can't at the same time do *that*; and if you do it to *these* men, you can't also do it to *those*. Hence from the outset the law of beneficence involves not doing some good to some men at some times. Hence those rules which so far as I know have never been doubted, as that we should help one we have promised to help rather than another, or a benefactor rather than one who has no special claims on us, or a compatriot more than a stranger, or a kinsman rather than a mere compatriot. And this in fact most often means helping A at the expense of B, who drowns while you pull A on board. And sooner or later, it involves helping A by actually doing some degree of violence to B. But when B is up to mischief against A, you must either do nothing (which disobeys the intuition) or you must help one against the other. And certainly no one's conscience tells him to help B, the guilty. It remains, therefore, to help A. So far, I suppose, we all agree. If the argument is not to end in an anti-Pacifist conclusion, one or other of two stopping places must be selected. You must either say that violence to B is lawful only if it stops short of killing, or else that killing of individuals is indeed lawful but the mass killing of a war is not.

As regards the first, I admit the general proposition that the lesser violence done to B is always preferable to the greater, provided that it is equally efficient in restraining him and equally good for everyone concerned, including B, whose claim is inferior to all the other claims involved but not nonexistent. But I do not therefore conclude that to kill B is always wrong. In some instances – for instance in a small, isolated community, death may be the only efficient method of restraint. In any community its effect on the population, not simply as a deterrent through fear, but also as an expression of the moral importance of certain crimes, may be valuable. And as for B himself, I think a bad man is at least as likely to make a good end in the execution shed some weeks after the crime as in the prison hospital twenty years later. I am not producing arguments to show that capital punishment is certainly right; I am only maintaining that it is not certainly wrong; it is a matter on which good men may legitimately differ.

As regards the second, the position seems to be much clearer. It is arguable that a criminal can always be satisfactorily dealt with without the death penalty. It is certain that a whole nation cannot be prevented from taking what it wants except by war. It is almost equally certain that the absorption of certain societies by certain other societies is a greater evil. The doctrine that war is always a great evil seems to imply a materialist ethic, a belief that death and pain are the greatest evils. But I do not think they are. I think the suppression of a higher religion by a lower, or even a higher secular culture by a lower, a much greater evil. Nor am I greatly moved by the fact that many of the individuals we strike down in war are innocent. That seems, in a way, to make war not worse but better. All men die, and most men miserably. That two soldiers on opposite sides, each believing his own country to be in the right, each at the moment when his selfishness is most in abeyance and his will to sacrifice in the ascendant, should kill each other in plain battle seems to me by no means one of the most terrible things in this very terrible world. Of course, one of them (at least) must be mistaken. And of course war is a very great evil. But that is not the question. The question is whether war is the greatest evil in the world, so that any state of affairs which might result from submission is certainly preferable. And I do not see any really cogent arguments for that view.

Another attempt to get a Pacifist conclusion from the intuition is of a more political and calculating kind. If not the greatest evil, yet war is a great evil. Therefore, we should all like to remove it if we can. But every war leads to another war. The removal of war must therefore be attempted. We must increase by propaganda the number of Pacifists in each nation until it becomes great enough to deter that nation from going to war. This seems to me wild work. Only liberal societies tolerate Pacifists. In the liberal society, the number of Pacifists will either be large enough to cripple the state as a belligerent, or not. If not, you have done nothing. If it is large enough, then you have handed over the state which does tolerate Pacifists to its totalitarian neighbour who does not. Pacifism of this kind is taking the straight road to a world in which there will be no Pacifists.

It may be asked whether, faint as the hope is of abolishing

war by Pacifism, there is any other hope. But the question belongs to a mode of thought which I find quite alien to me. It consists in assuming that the great permanent miseries in human life must be curable if only we can find the right cure; and it then proceeds by elimination and concludes that whatever is left, however unlikely to prove a cure, must nevertheless do so. Hence the fanaticism of Marxists, Freudians, Eugenists, Spiritualists, Douglasites, Federal Unionists, Vegetarians, and all the rest. But I have received no assurance that anything we can do will eradicate suffering. I think the best results are obtained by people who work quietly away at their objectives, such as the abolition of the slave trade, or prison reform, or factory acts, or tuberculosis, not by those who think they can achieve universal justice, or health, or peace. I think the art of life consists in tackling each immediate evil as well as we can. To avert or postpone one particular war by wise policy, or to render one particular campaign shorter by strength and skill or less terrible by mercy to the conquered and the civilians, is more useful than all the proposals for universal peace that have ever been made; just as the dentist who can stop one toothache has deserved better of humanity than all the men who think they have some scheme for producing a perfectly healthy race.

I do not therefore find any very clear and cogent reason for inferring from the general principle of beneficence the conclusion that I must disobey if I am called on by lawful authority to be a soldier. I turn next to consider Authority. Authority is either special or general, and again either human or divine.

The special human authority which rests on me in this matter is that of the society to which I belong. That society by its declaration of war has decided the issue against Pacifism in this particular instance, and by its institutions and practice for centuries has decided against Pacifism in general. If I am a Pacifist, I have Arthur and Aelfred, Elizabeth and Cromwell, Walpole and Burke, against me. I have my university, my school, and my parents against me. I have the literature of my country against me, and cannot even open my *Beowulf*, my Shakespeare, my Johnson or my Wordsworth without being reproved. Now, of course, this authority of England is not final. But there is a difference between conclusive authority and authority of no weight at all. Men may differ as to the weight they would give the almost unanimous authority of England. I am not here concerned with assessing it but merely with noting that whatever weight it has is against Pacifism. And, of course, my duty to take that authority into account is increased by the fact that I am indebted to that society for my birth and my upbringing, for the education which has allowed me to become a Pacifist, and the tolerant laws which allow me to remain one.

So much for special human authority. The sentence of general human authority is equally clear. From the dawn of history down to the sinking of the *Terris Bay*, the world echoes with the praise of righteous war. To be a Pacifist, I must part company with Homer and Virgil, with Plato and Aristotle, with Zarathustra and the *Bhagavad-Gita*, with Cicero and Montaigne, with Iceland and with Egypt. From this point of view, I am almost tempted to reply to the Pacifist as Johnson replied to Goldsmith, "Nay Sir, if you will not take the universal opinion of mankind, I have no more to say."

I am aware that, though Hooker thought "the general and perpetual voice of men is as the sentence of God Himself", yet many who hear will give it little or no weight. This disregard of human authority may have two roots. It may spring from the belief that human history is a simple, unilinear movement from worse to better – what is called a belief in Progress – so that any given generation is always in all respects wiser than all previous generations. To those who believe thus, our ancestors are superseded and there seems nothing improbable in the claim that the whole world was wrong until the day before yesterday and now has suddenly become right. With such people I confess I cannot argue, for I do not share their basic assumption. Believers in progress rightly note that in the world of machines the new model supersedes the old; from this they falsely infer a similar kind of supercession in such things as virtue and wisdom.

But human authority may be discounted on a quite different ground. It may be held, at least by a Christian Pacifist, that the human race is fallen and corrupt, so that even the consent of great and wise human teachers and great nations widely separated in time and place affords no clue whatsoever to the good. If this contention is being made, we must then turn to our next head, that of Divine Authority.

I shall consider Divine Authority only in terms of Christianity. Of the other civilized religions I believe that only one – Buddhism – is genuinely Pacifist; and anyway I am not well enough informed about them to discuss them with profit. And when we turn to Christianity, we find Pacifism based almost exclusively on certain of the sayings of Our Lord Himself. If those sayings do not establish the Pacifist position, it is vain to try to base it on the general *securus judicat* of Christendom as a whole. For when I seek guidance there, I find Authority on the whole against me. Looking at the statement which is my immediate authority as an Anglican, the Thirty-Nine Articles, I find it laid down in black and white that "it is lawful for Christian men, at the commandment of the Magistrate, to wear weapons and serve in the wars". Dissenters may not accept this; then I can refer them to the history of the Presbyterians, which is by no means Pacifist. Papists may not accept this; then I can refer them to the ruling of Thomas Aquinas that "even as princes lawfully defend their land by the sword against disturbance from within, so it belongs to them to defend it by the sword from enemies without." Or if you demand patristic authority, I give you St Augustine, "If Christian discipleship wholly reprobated war, then to those who sought the counsel of salvation in the Gospel this answer would have been given first, that they should throw away their arms and withdraw themselves altogether from being soldiers. But what was really said to them was, 'Do violence to no man and be content with your pay'. When he bade them to be content with their due soldiers' pay, he forbade them not to be paid as soldiers." But of checking individual voices, there would be no end. All bodies that claim to be Churches – that is, who claim apostolic succession and accept the Creeds – have constantly blessed what they regarded as righteous arms. Doctors, bishops and popes – including, I think, the present Pope [Pius XII] – have again and again discountenanced the Pacifist position. Nor, I think, do we find a word about Pacifism in the apostolic writings, which are older than the gospels and represent, if anything does, that original Christendom whereof the gospels themselves are a product.

The whole Christian case for Pacifism rests, therefore, on certain Dominical utterances, such as "Resist not evil: but whosoever shall smite thee on thy right cheek, turn to him the other also." I am now to deal with the Christian who says this is to be taken without qualification. I need not point out – for it has doubtless been pointed out to you before – that such a Christian is obliged to take all the other hard sayings of Our Lord in the same way. For the man who has done so, who has on every occasion given to all who ask him and has finally given all he has to the poor, no one will fail to feel respect. With such a man I must suppose myself to be arguing; for who would deem worth answering that inconsistent person who takes Our Lord's words *à la rigueur* when they dispense him from a possible obligation, and takes them with latitude when they demand that he should become a pauper?

There are three ways of taking the command to turn the other cheek. One is the Pacifist interpretation; it means what it says and imposes a duty of non-resistance on all men in all circumstances. Another is the minimizing interpretation; it does not mean what it says but is merely an orientally hyperbolical way of saying that you should put up with a lot and be placable. Both you and I agree in rejecting this view. The conflict is therefore between the Pacifist interpretation and a third one which I am now going to propound. I think the text means exactly what it says, but with an understood reservation in favour of those obviously exceptional cases which every hearer would naturally assume to be exceptions without being told. Or to put the same thing in more logical language, I think the duty of non-resistance is here stated as regards injuries *simpliciter*, but without prejudice to anything we may have to allow later about injuries *secundum quid*. That is, in so far as the only relevant factors in the case are an injury to me by my neighbour and a desire on my part to retaliate, then I hold that Christianity commands the absolute mortification of that desire. No quarter whatever is given to the voice within us which says, "He's done it to me, so I'll do the same to him". But the moment you introduce other factors, of course, the problem is altered. Does anyone suppose that Our Lord's hearers understood Him to mean that if a homicidal maniac, attempting to murder a third party, tried to knock me out of the way, I must stand aside and let him get his victim? I at any rate think it impossible they could have so understood Him. I think it equally impossible that they supposed Him to mean that the best way of bringing up a child was to let it hit its parents whenever it was in a temper, or, when it had grabbed at the jam, to give it the honey also. I think the meaning of the words was perfectly clear – "In so far as you are simply an angry man who has been hurt, mortify your anger and do not hit back" – even, one would have assumed that in so far as you are a magistrate struck by a private person, a parent struck by a child, a teacher by a scholar, a sane man by a lunatic, or a soldier by the public enemy, your duties may be very different, different because they may be then other motives than egoistic retaliation for hitting back. Indeed, as the audience were private people in a disarmed nation, it seems unlikely that they would have ever supposed Our Lord to be referring to war. War was not what they would have been thinking of. The frictions of daily life among villagers were more likely to be in their minds.

That is my chief reason for preferring this interpretation to yours. Any saying is to be taken in the sense it would naturally have borne in the time and place of utterance. But I also think that, so taken, it harmonizes better with St John Baptist's words to the soldiers, and with the fact that one of the few persons whom Our Lord praised without reservation was a Roman centurion. It also allows me to suppose that the New Testament is consistent with itself. St Paul approves of the magistrate's use of the sword (Romans 13:4) and so does St Peter (1 Peter 2:14). If Our Lord's words are taken in the unqualified sense which the Pacifist demands, we shall then be forced to the conclusion that Christ's true meaning, concealed from those who lived in the same time and spoke the same language, and whom He Himself chose to be His messengers to the world, as well as from all their successors, has at last been discovered in our own time. I know there are people who will not find this sort of thing difficult to believe, just as there are people ready to maintain that the true meaning of Plato or

Shakespeare, oddly concealed from their contemporaries and immediate successors, has preserved its virginity for the daring embraces of one or two modern professors. But I cannot apply to divine matters a method of exegesis which I have already rejected with contempt in my profane studies. Any theory which bases itself on a supposed "historical Jesus", to be dug out of the gospels and then set up in opposition to Christian teaching, is suspect. There have been too many historical Jesuses – a liberal Jesus, a pneumatic Jesus, a Barthian Jesus, a Marxist Jesus. They are the cheap crop of each publisher's list, like the new Napoleons and new Queen Victorias. It is not to such phantoms that I look for my faith and my salvation.

Christian authority, then, fails me in my search for Pacifism. It remains to inquire whether, if I still remain a Pacifist, I ought to suspect the secret influence of any passion. I hope you will not here misunderstand me. I do not intend to join in any of the jibes to which those of your persuasion are exposed in the popular press. Let me say at the outset that I think it unlikely there is anyone present less courageous than myself. But let me also say that there is no man alive so virtuous that he need feel himself insulted at being asked to consider the possibility of a warping passion when the choice is one between so much happiness and so much misery. For let us make no mistake. All that we fear from all the kinds of adversity, severally, is collected together in the life of a soldier on active service. Like sickness, it threatens pain and death. Like poverty, it threatens ill lodging, cold, heat, thirst and hunger. Like slavery, it threatens toil, humiliation, injustice and arbitrary rule. Like exile, it separates you from all you love. Like the galleys, it imprisons you at close quarters with uncongenial companions. It threatens *every* temporal evil – every evil except dishonour and final perdition, and those who bear it like it no better than you would like it. On the other side, though it may not be your fault, it is certainly a fact that Pacifism threatens you with almost nothing. Some public opprobrium, yes, from people whose opinion you discount and whose society you do not frequent, soon recompensed by the warm mutual approval which exists, inevitably, in any minority group. For the rest it offers you a continuance of the life you know and love, among the people and in the surroundings you know and love. It offers you time to lay the foundations of a career; for whether you will or no, you can hardly help getting the jobs for which the discharged soldiers will one day look in vain. You do not even have to fear, as Pacifists may have had to fear in the last war, that public opinion will punish you when the peace comes. For we have learned now that though the world is slow to forgive, it is quick to forget.

This, then, is why I am not a Pacifist. If I tried to become one, I should find a very doubtful factual basis, an obscure train of reasoning, a weight of authority both human and Divine against me, and strong grounds for suspecting that my wishes had directed my decision. As I have said, moral decisions do not admit of mathematical certainty. It may be, after all, that Pacifism is right. But it seems to me very long odds, longer odds than I would care to take with the voice of almost all humanity against me.

4

The Pains of Animals
A Problem in Theology[1]

(1950)

The Inquiry by C.E.M. Joad

For many years the problem of pain and evil seemed to me to offer an insuperable objection to Christianity. Either God could abolish them but did not, in which case, since He deliberately tolerated the presence in the universe of a state of affairs which was bad, I did not see how He could be good; or He wanted to abolish them but could not, in which case I did not see how He could be all-powerful. The dilemma is as old as St Augustine, and nobody pretends that there is an easy way of escape.

Moreover, all the attempts to explain pain away, or to mitigate its stark ferocity, or to present it as other than a very great evil, perhaps the greatest of evils, are palpable failures. They are testimonies to the kindness of men's hearts or perhaps to the queasiness of their consciences, rather than to the sharpness of their wits.

And yet, granting pain to be an evil, perhaps the greatest of evils, I have come to accept the Christian view of pain as not incompatible with the Christian concept of the Creator and of the world that He has made. That view I take to be

---

[1] In his book, *The Problem of Pain*, one of the questions Lewis addressed himself to was how to account for the occurrence of pain in a universe which is the creation of an all-good God, and in creatures who are not morally sinful. His chapter on "Animal Pain" provoked a counter-inquiry from the late C.E.M. Joad, who was Head of the Department of Philosophy in the University of London. The result was this controversy, first published in *The Month*

briefly as follows: It was of no interest to God to create a species consisting of virtuous automata, for the "virtue" of automata who can do no other than they do is a courtesy title only; it is analogous to the "virtue" of the stone that rolls downhill or of the water that freezes at 32°. To what end, it may be asked, should God create such creatures? That He might be praised by them? But automatic praise is a mere succession of noises. That He might love them? But they are essentially unlovable; you cannot love puppets. And so God gave man free will that he might increase in virtue by his own efforts and become, as a free moral being, a worthy object of God's love. Freedom entails freedom to go wrong: man did, in fact, go wrong, misusing God's gift and doing evil. Pain is a by-product of evil; and so pain came into the world as a result of man's misuse of God's gift of free will.

So much I can understand; so much, indeed, I accept. It is plausible; it is rational; it hangs together.

But now I come to a difficulty, to which I see no solution; indeed, it is in the hope of learning of one that this article is written. This is the difficulty of animal pain, and, more particularly, of the pain of the animal world before man appeared upon the cosmic scene. What account do theologians give of it? The most elaborate and careful account known to me is that of C.S. Lewis.

He begins by making a distinction between sentience and consciousness. When we have the sensations *a*, *b* and *c*, the fact that we have them and the fact that we know that we have them imply that there is something which stands sufficiently outside them to notice that they occur and that they succeed one another. This is consciousness, the consciousness to which the sensations happen. In other words, the experience of succession, the succession of sensations, demands a self or soul which is other than the sensations which it experiences. (Mr Lewis invokes the helpful metaphor of the bed of a river along which the stream of sensations flows.) Consciousness, therefore, implies a continuing *ego* which recognizes the succession of sensations; sentience is their mere succession. Now animals have sentience but not consciousness. Mr Lewis illustrates as follows:

> This would mean that if you give such a creature two blows with a whip, there are, indeed, two pains: but there is no co-ordinating self which can recognize that "I have had two pains". Even in the single pain there is no self to say "I am in pain" – for if it could distinguish itself from the sensation – the bed from the stream – sufficiently to say "I am in pain", it would also be able to connect the two sensations as *its* experience.[1]

(*a*) I take Mr Lewis's point – or, rather, I take it without perceiving its relevance. The question is how to account for the occurrence of pain (i) in a universe which is the creation of an all-good God; (ii) in creatures who are not morally sinful. To be told that the creatures are not really creatures, since they are not conscious in the sense of consciousness defined, does not really help matters. If it be true, as Mr Lewis says, that the right way to put the matter is not "This animal is feeling pain" but "Pain is taking place in this animal",[2] pain is nevertheless taking place. Pain is felt even if there is no continuing *ego* to feel it and to relate it to past and to future pains. Now it is the fact that pain is felt, no matter who or what feels it, or whether any continuing consciousness feels it, in a universe planned by a good God, that demands explanation.

(*b*) Secondly, the theory of sentience as mere succession of sensations presupposes that there is no continuing consciousness. No continuing consciousness presupposes no memory. It seems to me to be nonsense to say that animals do not remember. The dog who cringes at the sight of the whip by which he has been constantly beaten *behaves* as if he remembers, and behaviour is all that we have to go by. In general, we all act upon the assumption that the horse, the cat, and the dog with which we are acquainted remember very well, remember sometimes better than we do. Now I do not see how it is possible to explain the fact of memory without a continuing consciousness.

Mr Lewis recognizes this and concedes that the higher animals – apes, elephants, dogs, cats and so on – have a self which connects experiences; have, in fact, what he calls a soul.[1] But this assumption presents us with a new set of difficulties.

(a) If animals have souls, what is to be done about their immortality? The question, it will be remembered, is elaborately debated in Heaven at the beginning of Anatole France's *Penguin Island* after the short-sighted St Mael has baptized the penguins, but no satisfactory solution is offered.

(b) Mr Lewis suggests that the higher domestic animals achieve immortality as members of a corporate society of which the head is man. It is, apparently, "The-goodman-and-the-goodwife-ruling-their-children-and-their-beasts-in-the-good-homestead"[2] who survive. "If you ask," he writes, "concerning an animal thus raised as a member of the whole Body of the homestead, where its personal identity resides, I answer, 'Where its identity always did reside even in the earthly life – in its relation to the Body and, specially, to the master who is the head of that Body.' In other words, the man will know his dog: the dog will know its master, and, in knowing him, will *be* itself."[3]

[1] ibid., p. 121
[2] ibid., p. 127
[3] ibid., p. 128

Whether this is good theology, I do not know, but to our present inquiry it raises two difficulties.

(i) It does not cover the case of the higher animals who do not know man – for example, apes and elephants – but who are yet considered by Mr Lewis to have souls.

(ii) If one animal may attain good immortal selfhood in and through a good man, he may attain bad immortal selfhood in and through a bad man. One thinks of the overnourished lapdogs of idle overnourished women. It is a a little hard that when, through no fault of their own, animals fall to selfish, self-indulgent, or cruel masters, they should through eternity form part of selfish, self-indulgent, or cruel superpersonal wholes and perhaps be punished for their participation in them.

(c) If the animals have souls and, presumably, freedom, the same sort of explanation must be adopted for pain in animals as is offered for pain in men. Pain, in other words, is one of the evils consequent upon sin. The higher animals, then, are corrupt. The question arises, who corrupted them? There seem to be two possible answers: (1) The Devil; (2) Man.

(1) Mr Lewis considers this answer. The animals, he says, may originally all have been herbivorous. They became carnivorous – that is to say, they began to prey upon, to tear, and to eat one another – because "some mighty created power had already been at work for ill on the material universe, or the solar system, or, at least, the planet Earth, before ever man came on the scene ... If there is such a power ... it may well have corrupted the animal creation before man appeared."[1]

I have three comments to make:

(i) I find the supposition of Satan tempting monkeys frankly incredible. This, I am well aware, is not a logical objection.

[1] ibid., pp. 122–3

It is one's imagination – or perhaps one's common sense? – that revolts against it.

(ii) Although most animals fall victims to the redness of nature's "tooth and claw", many do not. The sheep falls down the ravine, breaks its leg, and starves; hundreds of thousands of migrating birds die every year of hunger; creatures are struck and not killed by lightning, and their seared bodies take long to die. Are these pains due to corruption?

(iii) The case of animals without souls cannot, on Mr Lewis's own showing, be brought under the "moral corruption" explanation. Yet consider just one instance of nature's arrangements. The wasps, *Ichneumonidae*, sting their caterpillar prey in such a way as to paralyse its nerve centres. They then lay their eggs on the helpless caterpillar. When the grubs hatch from the eggs, they immediately proceed to feed upon the living but helpless flesh of their incubators, the paralysed but still sentient caterpillars.

It is hard to suppose that the caterpillar feels no pain when slowly consumed; harder still to ascribe the pain to moral corruption; hardest of all to conceive how such an arrangement could have been planned by an all-good and all-wise Creator.

(2) The hypothesis that the animals were corrupted by man does not account for animal pain during the hundreds of millions of years (probably about 900 million) when the earth contained living creatures but did not contain man.

In sum, either animals have souls or they have no souls. If they have none, pain is felt for which there can be no moral responsibility, and for which no misuse of God's gift of moral freedom can be invoked as an excuse. If they have souls, we can give no plausible account (*a*) of their immortality – how draw the line between animals with souls and men with souls? – or (*b*) of their moral corruption, which would enable Christian apologists to place them in respect of their pain under the same heading of explanation as that which is proposed and which I am prepared to accept for man.

It may well be that there is an answer to this problem. I would be grateful to anyone who would tell me what it is.

The Reply by C.S. Lewis

Though there is pleasure as well as danger in encountering so sincere and economical a disputant as Dr Joad, I do so with no little reluctance. Dr Joad writes not merely as a controversialist who demands, but as an inquirer who really desires, an answer. I come into the matter at all only because my answers have already failed to satisfy him. And it is embarrassing to me, and possibly depressing to him, that he should, in a manner, be sent back to the same shop which has once failed to supply the goods. If it were wholly a question of defending the original goods, I think I would let it alone. But it is not exactly that. I think he has perhaps slightly misunderstood what I was offering for sale.

Dr Joad is concerned with the ninth chapter of my *Problem of Pain*. And the first point I want to make is that no one would gather from his article how confessedly speculative that chapter was. This was acknowledged in my preface and repeatedly emphasized in the chapter itself. This, of course, can bring no ease to Dr Joad's difficulties; unsatisfactory answers do not become satisfactory by being tentative. I mention the character of the chapter to underline the fact that it stands on a rather different level from those which preceded it. And that difference suggests the place which my "guess-work" about Beasts (so I called it at the time and call it still) had in my own thought, and which I would like this whole question to have in Dr Joad's thought too.

The Pains of Animals

The first eight chapters of my book attempted to meet the *prima facie* case against Theism based on human pain. They were the fruit of a slow change of mind not at all unlike that which Dr Joad himself has undergone and to which, when it had been completed, he at once bore honourable and (I expect) costly witness. The process of his thought differed at many points (very likely for the better) from the process of mine. But we came out, more or less, at the same place. The position of which he says in his article "So much I understand; so much, indeed, I accept" is very close to that which I reached in the first eight chapters of my *Problem*.

So far, so good. Having "got over" the problem of human pain, Dr Joad and I both find ourselves faced with the problem of animal pain. We do not at once part company even then. We both (if I read him correctly) turn with distaste from "the easy speeches that comfort cruel men",[1] from theologians who do not seem to see that there is a real problem, who are content to say that animals are, after all, only animals. To us, pain without guilt or moral fruit, however low and contemptible the sufferer may be, is a very serious matter.

I now ask Dr Joad to observe rather closely what I do at this point, for I doubt if it is exactly what he thinks. I do not advance a doctrine of animal sentience as proved and thence conclude. "Therefore beasts are not sacrificed without recompense, and therefore God is just." If he will look carefully at my ninth chapter he will see that it can be divided into two very unequal parts: Part One consisting of the first paragraph, and Part Two of all the rest. They might be summarized as follows:

Part One. The data which God has given us enable us in some degree to understand human pain. We lack such data

[1] G.K. Chesterton, "A Hymn", line 11. The first line begins "O God of earth and altar"

about beasts. We know neither what they are nor why they are. All that we can say for certain is that if God is good (and I think we have grounds for saying that He is) then the appearance of divine cruelty in the animal world must be a false appearance. What the reality behind the false appearance may be we can only guess.

Part Two. And here are some of my own guesses.

Now it matters far more whether Dr Joad agrees with Part One than whether he approves any of the speculations in Part Two. But I will first deal, so far as I can, with his critique of the speculations.

(1) Conceding (*positionis causa*)[1] my distinction between sentience and consciousness, Dr Joad thinks it irrelevant. "Pain is felt", he writes, "even if there is no continuing *ego* to feel it and to relate it to past and future pain", and "it is the fact that pain is felt, no matter who or what feels it . . . that demands explanation." I agree that in one sense it does not (for the present purpose) matter "who or what" feels it. That is, it does not matter how humble, or helpless, or small, or how removed from our spontaneous sympathies, the sufferer is. But it surely does matter how far the sufferer is capable of what we can recognize as misery, how far the genuinely pitiable is consistent with its mode of existence. It will hardly be denied that the more coherently conscious the subject is, the more pity and indignation its pains deserve. And this seems to me to imply that the less coherently conscious, the less they deserve. I still think it possible for there to be a pain so instantaneous (through the absence of all perception of succession) that its "unvalue", if I may coin the word, is indistinguishable from zero. A correspondent has instanced shooting pains in our own experience on those occasions when they are unaccompanied by fear. They may be intense: but they are

[1] for the sake of argument

gone as we recognize their intensity. In my own case I do not find anything in them which demands pity; they are, rather, comical. One tends to laugh. A series of such pains is, no doubt, terrible; but then the contention is that the series could not exist for sentience without consciousness.

(2) I do not think that behaviour "as if from memory" proves memory in the conscious sense. A non-human observer might suppose that if we blink our eyes at the approach of an object we are "remembering" pains received on previous occasions. But no memories, in the full sense, are involved. (It is, of course, true that the behaviour of the organism is modified by past experiences, and we may thus by metonymy say that the nerves remember what the mind forgets; but that is not what Dr Joad and I are talking of.) If we are to suppose memory in all cases where behaviour adapts itself to a probable recurrence of past events, shall we not have to assume in some insects an inherited memory of their parents' breeding habits? And are we prepared to believe this?

(3) Of course my suggested theory of the tame animals' resurrection "in" its human (and therefore, indirectly, divine) context does not cover wild animals or ill-treated tame ones. I had made the point myself, and added "it is intended only as an illustration . . . of the general principles to be observed in framing a theory of animal resurrection".[1] I went on to make an alternative suggestion, observing, I hope, the same principles. My chief purpose at this stage was at once to liberate imagination and to confirm a due agnosticism about the meaning and destiny of brutes. I had begun by saying that if our previous assertion of divine goodness was sound, we might be sure that *in some way or other* "all would be well, and all manner of thing would be well".[2] I wanted to reinforce this by indicating how little we

[1] *The Problem of Pain*, p. 128
[2] Lady Julian of Norwich, *Sixteenth Revelations of Divine Love*, ch. 29

knew and, therefore, how many things one might keep in mind as possibilities.

(4) If Dr Joad thinks I pictured Satan "tempting monkeys", I am myself to blame for using the word "encouraged". I apologize for the ambiguity. In fact, I had not supposed that "temptation" (that is, solicitation of the will) was the only mode in which the Devil could corrupt or impair. It is probably not the only mode in which he can impair even human beings; when Our Lord spoke of the deformed woman as one "bound by Satan",[1] I presume He did not mean that she had been tempted into deformity. Moral corruption is not the only kind of corruption. But the word *corruption* was perhaps ill-chosen and invited misunderstanding. *Distortion* would have been safer.

(5) My correspondent writes "that even the severest injuries in most invertebrate animals are almost if not quite painless is the view of most biologists. Loeb collected much evidence to show that animals without cerebral hemispheres were indistinguishable from plants in every psychological respect. The instance readily occurs of the caterpillars which serenely go on eating though their interiors are being devoured by the larvae of some ichneumon fly. The Vivisection Act does not apply to invertebrates; which indicates the views of those who framed it."

(6) Though Dr Joad does not raise the point, I cannot forbear adding some most interesting suggestions about animal fear from the same correspondent. He points out that human fear contains two elements: (*a*) the physical sensations, due to the secretions, etc.; (*b*) the mental images of what will happen if one loses hold, or if the bomb falls here, or if the train leaves the rails. Now (*a*), in itself, is so far from being an unmixed grief, that when we

[1] Luke 13:16

can get it without (*b*), or with unbelieved (*b*), or even with subdued (*b*), vast numbers of people like it: hence switchbacks, water-shoots, fast motoring, mountain climbing.

But all this is nothing to a reader who does not accept Part One in my ninth chapter. No man in his senses is going to start building up a theodicy with speculations about the minds of beasts as his foundation. Such speculations are in place only, as I said, to open the imagination to possibilities and to deepen and confirm our inevitable agnosticism about the reality, and only after the ways of God *to Man* have ceased to seem unjustifiable. We do not know the answer: these speculations were guesses at what it might possibly be. What really matters is the argument that there must be an answer: the argument that if, in our own lives, where alone (if at all) we know Him, we come to recognize the *pulchritudo tam antiqua et tam nova*,[1] then, in other realms where we cannot know Him (*connaître*), though we may know (*savoir*) some few things about Him – then, despite appearances to the contrary, He cannot be a power of darkness. For there were appearances to the contrary in our own realm too; yet, for Dr Joad as for me, they have somehow been got over.

I know that there are moments when the incessant continuity and desperate helplessness of what at least seems to be animal suffering makes every argument for Theism sound hollow, and when (in particular) the insect world appears to be Hell itself visibly in operation around us. Then the old indignation, the old pity arises. But how strangely ambivalent this experience is: I need not expound the ambivalence at much length, for I think I have done so elsewhere, and I am sure that Dr Joad had long discerned it for himself. If I regard this pity and

[1] Beauty so ancient and so new, St Augustine, *Confessions*, Bk. X, ch. 27

indignation simply as subjective experiences of my own with no validity beyond their strength at the moment (which next moment will change), I can hardly use them as standards whereby to arraign the creation. On the contrary, they become strong as arguments against God just in so far as I take them to be transcendent illuminations to which creation must conform or be condemned. They are arguments against God only if they are themselves the voice of God. The more Shelleyan, the more Promethean my revolt, the more surely it claims a divine sanction. That the mere contingent Joad or Lewis, born in an era of secure and liberal civilization and imbibing from it certain humanitarian sentiments, should happen to be offended by suffering – what is that to the purpose? How will one base an argument for or against God on such an historical accident?

No. Not in so far as we feel these things, but in so far as we claim to be right in feeling them, in so far as we are sure that these standards have an empire *de jure* over all possible worlds, so far, and so far only, do they become a ground for disbelief – and at the same moment, for belief. God within us steals back at the moment of our condemning the apparent God without. Thus in Tennyson's poem the man who had become convinced that the God of his inherited creed was evil exclaimed: "If there be such a God, may the Great God curse him and bring him to nought."[1] For if there is no "Great God" behind the curse who curses? Only a puppet of the little apparent "God". His very curse is poisoned at the root: it is just the same sort of event as the very cruelties he is condemning, part of the meaningless tragedy.

[1] "Despair", 19, 106

From this I see only two exits: either that there is a Great God, and also a "God of this world",[1] a prince of the powers of the air, whom the Great God does curse, and sometimes curse through us; or else that the operations of the Great God are not what they seem to me to be.

5

The Founding of the
Oxford Socratic Club[1]

(1943)

Like a quietly efficient nurse arriving in a house confused
by illness, or like the new general arriving at the siege of
Ismail in Byron's *Don Juan*, our Chairman[2] broke in (if she
will pardon the word) during the autumn of 1941 on that
welter of discussion which even in wartime makes up
five-eighths of the night life of the Oxford undergraduate.
By stages which must have been very swift (for I cannot
remember them), we found that a new society had been
formed, that it was attempting the difficult programme of
meeting once a week,[3] that it was actually carrying this
programme out, that its numbers were increasing, and that
neither foul weather nor crowded rooms (they were lucky
who found seats even on the floor) would reduce the size of
the meetings. This was the Socratic Club. Socrates had
exhorted men to "follow the argument wherever it led
them": the Club came into existence to apply his principle
to one particular subject-matter – the *pros* and *cons* of the
Christian religion.

  It is a little remarkable that, to the best of my
knowledge, no society had ever before been formed for
such a purpose. There had been plenty of organizations

---

[1] This is Lewis's Preface to the first *Socratic Digest* (Oxford, 1942–43).
   Lewis was the Society's President from the time of its first meeting until
   he went to Cambridge in 1955
[2] Miss Stella Aldwinckle
[3] The first meeting was in Somerville College, Oxford, on 26th January
   1942

that were explicitly Christian – the S.C.M.,[1] the Ark,[2] the O.U.C.U.,[3] the O.I.C.C.U.[4] – and there had been plenty of others, scientific or political, which were if not explicitly, yet profoundly anti-Christian in outlook. The question about Christianity arose, no doubt, often enough in private conversation, and cast its shadow over the aesthetic or philosophical debates in many societies: but an arena specially devoted to the conflict between Christian and unbeliever was a novelty. Its value from a merely cultural point of view is very great. In any fairly large and talkative community such as a university there is always the danger that those who think alike should gravitate together into *coteries* where they will henceforth encounter opposition only in the emasculated form of rumour that the outsiders say thus and thus. The absent are easily refuted, complacent dogmatism thrives, and differences of opinion are embittered by group hostility. Each group hears not the best, but the worst, that the other groups can say. In the Socratic all this was changed. Here a man could get the case for Christianity without all the paraphernalia of pietism and the case against it without the irrelevant *sansculottisme* of our common anti-God weeklies. At the very least we helped to civilize one another; sometimes we ventured to hope that if our Athenian patron were allowed to be present, unseen, at our meetings he might not have found the atmosphere wholly alien.

We also learned, in those motley – and usually stifling – assemblies where English boys fresh from public schools rubbed shoulders with elderly European *Gelehrten* in exile, almost any type of opinion might turn up. Everyone found

[1] The Student Christian Movement
[2] An Oxford Christian society
[3] Oxford University Church Union
[4] Oxford Intercollegiate Christian Union, now called The Christian Union

how little he had known about everyone else. We of the Christian party discovered that the weight of the sceptical attack did not always come where we expected it; our opponents had to correct what seemed to us their almost bottomless ignorance of the Faith they supposed themselves to be rejecting.

It is (theoretically) a difficulty in the British Constitution that the Speaker of the House of Commons must himself be a member of one of the Parties. There is a similar difficulty about the Socratic. Those who founded it do not for one moment pretend to be neutral. It was the Christians who constructed the arena and issued the challenge. It will therefore always be possible for the lower (the less Athenian) type of unbeliever to regard the whole thing as a cunningly – or not even so very cunningly – disguised form of propaganda. The Athenian type, if he had this objection to make, would put it in a paper and read that paper to the Socratic itself. He would be welcome to do so – though I doubt whether he would have the stomach if he knew with what pains and toil the committee has scoured *Who's Who* to find intelligent atheists who had leisure or zeal to come and propagate their creed. But when all is said and done, the answer to any such suspicion lies deeper. It is not here that the honesty of the Socratic comes in. We never claimed to be impartial. But argument is. It has a life of its own. No man can tell where it will go. We expose ourselves, and the weakest of our party, to your fire no less than you are exposed to ours. Worse still, we expose ourselves to the recoil from our own shots; for if I may trust my personal experience no doctrine is, for the moment, dimmer to the eye of faith than that which a man has just successfully defended. The arena is common to both parties and cannot finally be cheated; in it you risk nothing, and we risk all.

Others may have quite a different objection to our proceedings. They may protest that intellectual discussion can neither build Christianity nor destroy it. They may feel that religion is too sacred to be thus bandied to and fro in public debate, too sacred to be talked of – almost, perhaps, too sacred for anything to be done with it all. Clearly the Christian members of the Socratic think differently. They know that intellectual assent is not faith, but they do not believe that religion is only "what a man does with his solitude". Or, if it is, then they care nothing for "religion" and all for Christianity. Christianity is not merely what a man does with his solitude. It is not even what God does with His solitude. It tells of God descending into the coarse publicity of history and there enacting what can – and must – be talked about.

6

Religion Without Dogma?[1]

(1946)

In his paper on "The Grounds of Modern Agnosticism", Professor Price maintains the following positions: (1) That the essence of religion is belief in God and immortality; (2) that in most actual religions the essence is found in connection with "accretions of dogma and mythology"[2] which have been rendered incredible by the progress of science; (3) that it would be very desirable, if it were possible, to retain the essence purged of the accretions; but (4) that science has rendered the essence almost as hard to believe as the accretions. For the doctrine of immortality involves the dualistic view that man is a composite creature, a soul in a state of symbiosis with a physical organism. But in so far as science can successfully regard man monistically, as a single organism whose psychological properties all arise from his physical, the soul becomes an indefensible hypothesis. In conclusion, Professor Price found our only hope in certain empirical evidence for the soul which

---

[1] This paper was originally read to the Oxford Socratic Club on 20th May 1946, in answer to a paper of Professor H.H. Price on "The Grounds of Modern Agnosticism" on 20th October 1944. Both were later published in the *Phoenix Quarterly* (Autumn 1946). Though Lewis's paper was afterwards reprinted in *The Socratic Digest* (1948), it is obvious from the fact that many errors which appear in the *Socratic* version were corrected in the *Quarterly* version, that the *Quarterly* version represents Lewis's final revision. Besides this, I have incorporated in the text given here all the marginal emendations and additions which Lewis made in his own copy of the *Phoenix Quarterly*.

[2] H.H. Price, "The Grounds of Modern Agnosticism", *Phoenix Quarterly*, Vol. I, No. 1 (Autumn 1946), p. 25

appears to him satisfactory; in fact, in the findings of Psychical Research.

My disagreement with Professor Price begins, I am afraid, at the threshold. I do not define the essence of religion as belief in God and immortality. Judaism in its earlier stages had no belief in immortality, and for a long time no belief which was religiously relevant. The shadowy existence of the ghost in Sheol was one of which Jehovah took no account and which took no account of Jehovah. In Sheol all things are forgotten. The religion was centred on the ritual and ethical demands of Jehovah in the present life, and also, of course, on benefits expected from Him. These benefits are often merely worldly benefits (grandchildren, and peace upon Israel), but a more specifically religious note is repeatedly struck. The Jew is athirst for the living God,[1] he delights in His Laws as in honey or treasure,[2] he is conscious of himself in Jehovah's presence as unclean of lips and heart.[3] The glory or splendour of the god is worshipped for its own sake. In Buddhism, on the other hand, we find that a doctrine of immortality is central, while there is nothing specifically religious. Salvation from immortality, deliverance from reincarnation, is the very core of its message. The existence of the gods is not necessarily decried, but it is of no religious significance. In Stoicism again both the religious quality and the belief in immortality are variables, but they do not vary in direct ratio. Even within Christianity itself we find a striking expression, not without influence from Stoicism, of the subordinate position of immortality. When Henry More ends a poem on the spiritual life by saying that if, after all, he should turn out to be mortal he would be

[1] Psalm 42:2
[2] Psalm 19:10
[3] Isaiah 6:5

...Satisfide
A lonesome mortal God t' have dide.[1]

From my own point of view, the examples of Judaism and
Buddhism are of immense importance. The system which is
meaningless without a doctrine of immortality regards immortality as a nightmare, not as a prize. The religion which,
of all ancient religions, is most specifically religious, that is,
at once most ethical and most numinous, is hardly interested
in the question. Believing as I do, that Jehovah is a real
being, indeed the *ens realissimum*, I cannot sufficiently
admire the divine tact of thus training the chosen race for
centuries in a religion before even hinting the shining secret
of eternal life. He behaves like the rich lover in a romance
who woos the maiden on his own merits, disguised as a poor
man, and only when he has won her reveals that he has a
throne and palace to offer. For I cannot help thinking that
any religion which begins with a thirst for immortality is
damned, as a religion, from the outset. Until a certain
spiritual level has been reached, the promise of immortality
will always operate as a bribe which vitiates the whole
religion and infinitely inflames those very self-regards which
religion must cut down and uproot. For the essence of
religion, in my view, is the thirst for an end higher than
natural ends; the finite self's desire for, and acquiescence in,
and self-rejection in favour of, an object wholly good and
wholly good for it. That the self-rejection will turn out to be
also a self-finding, that bread cast upon the waters will be
found after many days, that to die is to live – these are sacred
paradoxes of which the human race must not be told too
soon.

Differing from Professor Price about the essence of

---

[1] "Resolution", *The Complete Poems of Dr Henry More*, ed. Alexander
B. Grosart (Edinburgh, 1878), line 117, p. 176

religion, I naturally cannot, in a sense, discuss whether the essence as he defines it co-exists with accretions of dogma and mythology. But I freely admit that the essence as I define it always co-exists with other things; and that some of these other things even I would call mythology. But my list of things mythological would not coincide with his, and our views of mythology itself probably differ. A great many different views on it have, of course, been held. Myths have been accepted as literally true, then as allegorically true (by the Stoics), as confused history (by Euhemerus),[1] as priestly lies (by the philosophers of the Enlightenment), as imitative agricultural ritual mistaken for propositions (in the days of Frazer).[2] If you start from a naturalistic philosophy, then something like the view of Euhemerus or the view of Frazer is likely to result. But I am not a naturalist. I believe that in the huge mass of mythology which has come down to us a good many different sources are mixed – true history, allegory, ritual, the human delight in story telling, etc. But among these sources I include the supernatural, both diabolical and divine. We need here concern ourselves only with the latter. If my religion is erroneous then occurrences of similar motifs in pagan stories are, of course, instances of the same, or a similar, error. But if my religion is true, then these stories may well be a *preparatio evangelica*, divine hinting in poetic and ritual form at the same central truth which was later focused and (so to speak) historicized in the Incarnation. To me, who first approached Christianity from a delighted interest in, and reverence for, the best pagan imagination, who loved Balder before Christ and Plato before St Augustine, the anthropological argument against Christianity has never been formidable. On the contrary, I

---

[1] A Sicilian writer (*c.* 315 B.C.) who developed the theory that the ancient beliefs about the gods originated from the elaboration of traditions of actual historical persons

[2] James George Frazer, *The Golden Bough* (London, 1922)

could not believe Christianity if I were forced to say that there were a thousand religions in the world of which 999 were pure nonsense and the thousandth (fortunately) true. My conversion, very largely, depended on recognizing Christianity as the completion, the actualization, the entelechy, of something that had never been wholly absent from the mind of man. And I still think that the agnostic argument from similarities between Christianity and paganism works only if you know the answer. If you start by knowing on other grounds that Christianity is false, then the pagan stories may be another nail in its coffin: just as if you started by knowing that there were no such things as crocodiles then the various stories about dragons might help to confirm your disbelief. But if the truth or falsehood of Christianity is the very question you are discussing, then the argument from anthropology is surely a *petitio*.

There are, of course, many things in Christianity which I accept as fact and which Professor Price would regard as mythology. In a word, there are miracles. The contention is that science has proved that miracles cannot occur. According to Professor Price "a Deity who intervened miraculously and suspended natural law could never be accepted by Science";[1] whence he passes on to consider whether we cannot still believe in Theism without miracles. I am afraid I have not understood why the miracles could never be accepted by one who accepted science.

Professor Price bases his view on the nature of scientific method. He says that that method is based on two assumptions. The first is that all events are subject to laws, and he adds: "It does not matter for our purpose whether the laws are 'deterministic' or only 'statistical'."[2] But I submit that it matters to the scientist's view of the miraculous. The notion that natural laws may be merely

[1] Price, *op. cit.*, p. 20
[2] ibid.

statistical results from the modern belief that the individual unit of matter obeys no laws. Statistics were introduced to explain why, despite the lawlessness of the individual unit, the behaviour of gross bodies was regular. The explanation was that, by a principle well known to actuaries, the law of averages levelled out the individual eccentricities of the innumerable units contained in even the smallest gross body. But with this conception of the lawless units the whole impregnability of nineteenth-century Naturalism has, as it seems to me, been abandoned. What is the use of saying that all events are subject to laws if you also say that every event which befalls the individual unit of matter is *not* subject to laws. Indeed, if we define nature as the system of events in space-time governed by interlocking laws, then the new physics has really admitted that something other than nature exists. For if nature means the interlocking system then the behaviour of the individual unit is outside nature. We have admitted what may be called the sub-natural. After that admission what confidence is left us that there may not be a supernatural as well? It may be true that the lawlessness of the little events fed into nature from the sub-natural is always ironed out by the law of averages. It does not follow that great events could not be fed into her by the super-natural: nor that they also would allow themselves to be ironed out.

The second assumption which Professor Price attributes to the scientific method is "that laws can only be discovered by the study of publicly observable regularities".[1] Of course they can. This does not seem to me to be an assumption so much as a self-evident proposition. But what is it to the purpose? If a miracle occurs it is by definition an interruption of regularity. To discover a regularity is by definition not to discover its interruptions, even if they occur. You cannot discover a railway accident from studying

[1] ibid.

Bradshaw: only by being there when it happens or hearing about it afterwards from someone who was. You cannot discover extra half-holidays by studying a school timetable: you must wait till they are announced. But surely this does not mean that a student of Bradshaw is logically forced to deny the possibility of railway accidents. This point of scientific method merely shows (what no one to my knowledge ever denied) that if miracles *did* occur, science, as science, would not prove, or disprove, their occurrence. What cannot be trusted to recur is not material for science: that is why history is not one of the sciences. You cannot find out what Napoleon did at the battle of Austerlitz by asking him to come and fight it again in a laboratory with the same combatants, the same terrain, the same weather, and in the same age. You have to go to the records. We have not, in fact, proved that science excludes miracles: we have only proved that the question of miracles, like innumerable other questions, excludes laboratory treatment.

[1][If I thus hand over miracles from science to history (but not, of course, to historians who beg the question by beginning with materialistic assumptions) Professor Price thinks I shall not fare much better. Here I must speak with caution, for I do not profess to be a historian or a textual critic. I would refer you to Sir Arnold Lunn's book *The Third Day*.[2] If Sir Arnold is right, then the biblical criticism which began in the nineteenth century has already shot its bolt, and most of its conclusions have been successfully disputed, though it will, like nineteenth-century materialism, long continue to dominate popular thought. What I can say with more certainty is that that *kind* of criticism — the kind which discovers that every old book was

---

[1] In order that nothing should be lost to the reader, I have included between square brackets those portions from the *Socratic* version of this paper which Lewis omitted in revising it for the *Phoenix Quarterly*. See footnote p. 84

[2] (London, 1945)

made by six anonymous authors well provided with scissors and paste, and that every anecdote of the slightest interest is unhistorical, has already begun to die out in the studies I know best. The period of arbitrary scepticism about the canon and text of Shakespeare is now over: and it is reasonable to expect that this method will soon be used only on Christian documents and survive only in the *Thinkers' Library* and the theological colleges.]

I find myself, therefore, compelled to disagree with Professor Price's second point. I do not think that science has shown, or, by its nature, could ever show that the miraculous element in religion is erroneous. I am not speaking, of course, about the psychological effects of science on those who practise it or read its results. That the continued application of scientific methods breeds a temper of mind unfavourable to the miraculous, may well be the case, but even here there would seem to be some difference among the sciences. Certainly, if we think, not of the miraculous in particular, but of religion in general, there is such a difference. Mathematicians, astronomers and physicists are often religious, even mystical; biologists much less often; economists and psychologists very seldom indeed. It is as their subject matter comes nearer to man himself that their anti-religious bias hardens.

And that brings me to Professor Price's fourth point – for I would rather postpone consideration of his third. His fourth point, it will be remembered, was that science had undermined not only what he regards as the mythological accretions of religion, but also what he regards as its essence. That essence is for him Theism and immortality. In so far as natural science can give a satisfactory account of man as a purely biological entity, it excludes the soul and therefore excludes immortality. That, no doubt, is why the scientists who are most, or most nearly, concerned with man himself are the most anti-religious.

Now most assuredly if naturalism is right then it is at this point, at the study of man himself, that it wins its final victory and overthrows all our hopes: not only our hope of immortality, but our hope of finding significance in our lives here and now. On the other hand, if naturalism is wrong, it will be here that it will reveal its fatal philosophical defect, and that is what I think it does.

On the fully naturalistic view all events are determined by laws. Our logical behaviour, in other words our thoughts, and our ethical behaviour, including our ideals as well as our acts of will, are governed by biochemical laws; these, in turn, by physical laws which are themselves actuarial statements about the lawless movements of matter. These units never intended to produce the regular universe we see: the law of averages (successor to Lucretius's *exiguum clinamen*)[1] has produced it out of the collision of these random variations in movement. The physical universe never intended to produce organisms. The relevant chemicals on earth, and the sun's heat, thus juxtaposed, gave rise to this disquieting disease of matter: organization. Natural selection, operating on the minute differences between one organism and another, blundered into that sort of phosphorescence or mirage which we call consciousness — and that, in some cortexes beneath some skulls, at certain moments, still in obedience to physical laws, but to physical laws now filtered through laws of a more complicated kind, takes the form we call thought. Such, for instance, is the origin of this paper: such was the origin of Professor Price's paper. What we should speak of as his "thoughts" were merely the last link of a causal chain in which all the previous links were irrational. He spoke as he did because the matter of his brain was behaving in a certain way: and the whole history of the universe up to that moment had forced it to behave in that way. What we called his thought

[1] small inclination. *De Rerum Natura*, Bk. II, line 292

was essentially a phenomenon of the same sort as his other secretions – the form which the vast irrational process of nature was bound to take at a particular point of space and time.

Of course it did not feel like that to him or to us while it was going on. He appeared to himself to be studying the nature of things, to be in some way aware of the realities, even supersensuous realities, outside his own head. But if strict naturalism is right, he was deluded: he was merely enjoying the conscious reflection of irrationally determined events in his own head. It appeared to him that his thoughts (as he called them) could have to outer realities that wholly immaterial relation which we call truth or falsehood: though, in fact, being but the shadow of cerebral events, it is not easy to see that they could have any relations to the outer world except causal relations. And when Professor Price defended scientists, speaking of their devotion to truth and their constant following of the best light they knew, it seemed to him that he was choosing an attitude in obedience to an ideal. He did not feel that he was merely suffering a reaction determined by ultimately amoral and irrational sources, and no more capable of rightness or wrongness than a hiccup or a sneeze.

It would have been impossible for Professor Price to have written, or us to have read, his paper with the slightest interest if he and we had consciously held the position of strict naturalism throughout. But we can go further. It would be impossible to accept naturalism itself if we really and consistently believed naturalism. For naturalism is a system of thought. But for naturalism all thoughts are mere events with irrational causes. It is, to me at any rate, impossible to regard the thoughts which make up naturalism in that way and, at the same time, to regard them as a real insight into external reality. Bradley distinguished *idea-event* from *idea-making*,[1] but naturalism seems to me committed to regarding ideas simply as events. For meaning is a relation of a wholly new kind, as remote, as mysterious, as opaque to empirical study, as soul itself.

Perhaps this may be even more simply put in another way. Every particular thought (whether it is a judgement of fact or a judgement of value) is always and by all men discounted the moment they believe that it can be explained, without remainder, as the result of irrational causes. Whenever you know what the other man is saying is wholly due to his complexes or to a bit of bone pressing on his brain, you cease to attach any importance to it. But if naturalism were true then all thoughts whatever would be wholly the result of irrational causes. Therefore, all thoughts would be equally worthless. Therefore, naturalism is worthless. If it is true, then we can know no truths. It cuts its own throat.

[I remember once being shown a certain kind of knot which was such that if you added one extra complication to make assurance doubly sure you suddenly found that the whole thing had come undone in your hands and you had only a bit of string. It is like that with naturalism. It goes on claiming territory after territory: first the inorganic, then the lower organisms, then man's body, then his emotions. But when it takes the final step and we attempt a naturalistic account of thought itself, suddenly the whole thing unravels. The last fatal step has invalidated all the preceding ones: for they were all reasoning and reason itself has been discredited. We must, therefore, either give up thinking altogether or else begin over again from the ground floor.]

There is no reason, at this point, to bring in either Christianity or spiritualism. We do not need them to refute naturalism. It refutes itself. Whatever else we may come to believe about the universe, at least we cannot believe

---

[1] "Spoken and Written English", *The Collected Papers of Henry Bradley*, ed. Robert Bridges (Oxford, 1928), pp. 168–93.

naturalism. The validity of rational thought, accepted in an utterly non-naturalistic, transcendental (if you will), supernatural sense, is the necessary presupposition of all other theorizing. There is simply no sense in beginning with a view of the universe and trying to fit the claims of thought in at a later stage. By thinking at all we have claimed that our thoughts are more than mere natural events. All other propositions must be fitted in as best they can round that primary claim.

Holding that science has not refuted the miraculous element in religion, much less that naturalism, rigorously taken, can refute anything except itself, I do not, of course, share Professor Price's anxiety to find a religion which can do without what he calls the mythology. What he suggests is simple Theism, rendered credible by a belief in immortality which, in its turn, is guaranteed by Psychical Research. Professor Price is not, of course, arguing that immortality would of itself prove Theism: it would merely remove an obstacle to Theism. The positive source of Theism he finds in religious experience.

At this point it is very important to decide which of two questions we are asking. We may be asking: (1) whether this purged minimal religion suggested by Professor Price is capable, as a historical, social and psychological entity, of giving fresh heart to society, strengthening the moral will, and producing all those other benefits which, it is claimed, the old religions have sometimes produced. On the other hand, we may be asking: (2) whether this minimal religion will be the true one; that is, whether it contains the only true propositions we can make about ultimate questions.

The first question is not a religious question but a sociological one. The religious mind as such, like the older sort of scientific mind as such, does not care a rap about socially useful propositions. Both are athirst for reality, for the utterly objective, for that which is what it is. The "open mind" of the scientist and the emptied and silenced mind of the mystic are both efforts to eliminate what is our own in order that the Other may speak. And if, turning aside from the religious attitude, we speak for a moment as mere sociologists, we must admit that history does not encourage us to expect much envigorating power in a minimal religion. Attempts at such a minimal religion are not new – from Akhenaten [1] and Julian the Apostate[2] down to Lord Herbert of Cherbury[3] and the late H.G. Wells. But where are the saints, the consolations, the ecstasies? The greatest of such attempts was that simplification of Jewish and Christian traditions which we call Islam. But it retained many elements which Professor Price would regard as mythical and barbaric, and its culture is by no means one of the richest or most progressive.

Nor do I see how such a religion, if it became a vital force, would long be preserved in its freedom from dogma. Is its God to be conceived pantheistically, or after the Jewish, Platonic, Christian fashion? If we are to retain the minimal religion in all its purity, I suppose the right answer would be: "We don't know, and we must be content not to know." But that is the end of the minimal religion as a practical affair. For the question is of pressing practical importance. If the God of Professor Price's religion is an impersonal spirituality diffused through the whole universe, equally present, and present in the same mode, at all points of space and

[1] Akhenaton (Amenhotep IV), king of Egypt, who came to the throne about 1375 B.C. and introduced a new religion, in which the sun-god Ra (designated as "Aton") superseded Amon

[2] Roman emperor A.D. 361–3, who was brought up compulsorily as a Christian, but who on attaining the throne proclaimed himself a pagan. He made a great effort to revive the worship of the old gods

[3] Edward Herbert (1583–1648). He is known as the "Father of Deism", for he maintained that among the "common notions" apprehended by instinct are the existence of God, the duty of worship and repentance, and future rewards and punishment. This "natural religion", he maintained, had been vitiated by superstition and dogma

time, then He — or it — will certainly be conceived as being beyond good and evil, expressed equally in the brothel or the torture chamber and in the model factory or the university common room. If, on the other hand, He is a personal Being standing outside His creation, commanding this and prohibiting that, quite different consequences follow. The choice between these two views affects the choice between courses of action at every moment both in private and public life. Nor is this the only such question that arises. Does the minimal religion know whether its god stands in the same relation to all men, or is he related to some as he is not related to others? To be true to its undogmatic character it must again say: "Don't ask." But if that is the reply, then the minimal religion cannot exclude the Christian view that He was present in a special way in Jesus, nor the Nazi view that He is present in a special way in the German race, nor the Hindu view that He is specially present in the Brahmin, nor the central African view that He is specially present in the thigh-bone of a dead English Tommy.

All these difficulties are concealed from us as long as the minimal religion exists only on paper. But suppose it were somehow established all over what is left of the British Empire, and let us suppose that Professor Price has (most reluctantly and solely from a sense of duty) become its supreme head on earth. I predict that one of two things must happen: (1) In the first month of his reign he will find himself uttering his first dogmatic definition — he will find himself saying, for example: "No. God is not an amoral force diffused through the whole universe to whom suttee and temple prostitution are no more and no less acceptable than building hospitals and teaching children; he is a righteous creator, separate from his creation, who demands of you justice and mercy"; or (2) Professor Price will not reply. In the second case is it not clear what will happen? Those who have come to his minimal religion from Christianity will conceive God in the Jewish, Platonic, Christian way; those who have come from Hinduism will conceive Him pantheistically; and the plain men who have come from nowhere will conceive Him as a righteous Creator in their moments of moral indignation, and as a pantheistic God in their moments of self-indulgence. And the ex-Marxist will think He is specially present in the Proletariat, and the ex-Nazi will think he is specially present in the German people. And they will hold world conferences at which they all speak the same language and reach the most edifying agreement: but they will all mean totally different things. The minimal religion in fact cannot, while it remains minimal, be acted on. As soon as you *do* anything you have assumed one of the dogmas. In practice it will not be a religion at all; it will be merely a new colouring given to all the different things people were doing already.

[I submit it to Professor Price, with great respect, that when he spoke of mere Theism, he was all the time unconsciously assuming a particular conception of God: that is, he was assuming a dogma about God. And I do not think he was deducing it solely, or chiefly, from his own religious experience or even from a study of religious experience in general. For religious experience can be made to yield almost any sort of God. I think Professor Price assumed a certain sort of God because he has been brought up in a certain way: because Bishop Butler and Hooker and Thomas Aquinas and Augustine and St Paul and Christ and Aristotle and Plato are, as we say, "in his blood". He was not really starting from scratch. Had he done so, had God meant in his mind a being about whom no dogma whatever is held, I doubt whether he would have looked for even social salvation in such an empty concept. All the strength and value of the minimal religion, for him as for all others who accept it, is derived not from it, but from the tradition which he imports into it.]

The minimal religion will, in my opinion, leave us all doing what we were doing before. Now it, in itself, will not be an objection from Professor Price's point of view. He was not working for unity, but for some spiritual dynamism to see us through the black night of civilization. If Psychical Research has the effect of enabling people to continue, or to return to, all the diverse religions which naturalism has threatened, and if they can thus get power and hope and discipline, he will, I believe, leave us – as Western, mecha-nized, democratic, secularized men – exactly where we were. In what way will a belief in the immortality vouched for by Psychical Research, and in an unknown God, restore to us the virtue and energy of our ancestors? It seems to me that both beliefs, unless reinforced by something else, will be to modern man very shadowy and inoperative. If indeed we knew that God were righteous, that He had purposes for us, that He was the leader in a cosmic battle and that some real issue hung on our conduct in the field, then it would be something to the purpose. Or if, again, the utterances which purport to come from the other world ever had the accent which really *suggests* another world, ever spoke (as even the inferior actual religions do) with that voice before which our mortal nature trembles with awe or joy, then that also would be to the purpose. But the god of minimal Theism remains powerless to excite either fear or love: can be given power to do so only from those traditional resources to which, in Professor Price's conception, science will never permit our return. As for the utterances of the mediums . . . I do not wish to be offensive. But will even the most con-vinced spiritualist claim that one sentence from that source has ever taken its place among the golden sayings of man-kind, has ever approached (much less equalled) in power to elevate, strengthen or correct even the second rank of such sayings? Will anyone deny that the vast majority of spirit messages sink pitiably below the best that has been thought and said even in this world? – that in most of them we find a banality and provincialism, a paradoxical union of the prim with the enthusiastic, of flatness and gush, which would suggest that the souls of the moderately respectable are in the keeping of Annie Besant[1] and Martin Tupper?[2]

I am not arguing from the vulgarity of the messages that their claim to come from the dead is false. If I did the spiritualist would reply that this quality is due to imperfections in the medium of communication. Let it be so. We are not here discussing the truth of spiritualism, but its power to become the starting point of a religion. And for that purpose I submit that the poverty of its contents disqualifies it. A minimal religion compounded of spirit messages and bare Theism has no power to touch any of the deepest chords in our nature, or to evoke any response which will raise us even to a higher secular level – let alone to the spiritual life. The god of whom no dogmas are believed is a mere shadow. He will not produce that fear of the Lord in which wisdom begins, and, therefore, will not produce that love in which it is consummated. The immortality which the messages suggest can produce in mediocre spirits only a vague comfort for our unredeemedly personal hankerings, a shadowy sequel to the story of this world in which all comes right (but right in how pitiable a sense!), while the more spiritual will feel that it has added a new horror to death – the horror of mere endless succession, of indefinite imprisonment in that which binds us all, *das Gemeine*.[3] There is in this minimal religion nothing that can convince, convert, or (in the higher sense) console; nothing, therefore, which can

---

[1] Annie Besant (1847–1933) was an ardent supporter of Liberal causes and became a member of the Theosophical Society in 1889

[2] Martin Tupper (1810–89) is probably best known for his *Proverbial Philosophy* – commonplace maxims and reflections couched in a rhythmical form

[3] Johann Wolfgang Goethe, *Epilog zu Schillers Glocke*, 1. 32. "*Das Gemeine*" means something like "that which dominates us all"

restore vitality to our civilization. It is not costly enough. It can never be a controller or even a rival to our natural sloth and greed. A flag, a song, an old school tie, is stronger than it; much more, the pagan religions. Rather than pin my hopes on it I would almost listen again to the drum-beat in my blood (for the blood is at least in some sense the life) and join in the song of the Maenads:

> Happy they whom the Daimons
> Have befriended, who have entered
> The divine orgies, making holy
> Their life-days, till the dance throbs
> In their heart-beats, while they romp with
> Dionysus on the mountains . . .[1]

Yes, almost; I'd sooner be a pagan suckled in a creed outworn.

Almost, but not, of course, quite. If one is forced to such an alternative, it is perhaps better to starve in a wholly secularized and meaningless universe than to recall the obscenities and cruelties of paganism. They attract because they are a distortion of the truth, and therefore, retain some of its flavour. But with this remark I have passed into our second question. I shall not be expected at the end of this paper to begin an apologetic for the truth of Christianity. I will only say something which in one form or another I have said perhaps too often already. If there is no God then we have no interest in the minimal religion or any other. We will not make a lie even to save civilization. But if there is, then it is so probable as to be almost axiomatic that the initiative lies wholly on His side. If He can be known it will be by self-revelation on His part, not by speculation on ours. We, therefore, look for Him where it is claimed that He has revealed Himself by miracle, by inspired teachers, by

[1] Euripides, *Bacchae*, line 74

enjoined ritual. The traditions conflict, yet the longer and more sympathetically we study them the more we become aware of a common element in many of them: the theme of sacrifice, of mystical communion through the shed blood, of death and rebirth, of redemption, is too clear to escape notice. We are fully entitled to use moral and intellectual criticism. What we are not, in my opinion, entitled to do is simply to abstract the ethical element and set that up as a religion on its own. Rather in that tradition which is at once more completely ethical and most transcends mere ethics – in which the old themes of the sacrifice and re-birth recur in a form which transcends, though there it no longer revolts, our conscience and our reason – we may still most reasonably believe that we have the consummation of all religion, the fullest message from the wholly other, the living creator, who, if He is at all, must be the God not only of the philosophers, but of mystics and savages, not only of the head and heart, but also of the primitive emotions and the spiritual heights beyond all emotion. We may still reasonably attach ourselves to the Church, to the only concrete organization which has preserved down to this present time the core of all the messages, pagan and perhaps pre-pagan, that have ever come from beyond the world, and begin to practise the only religion which rests not upon some selection of certain supposedly "higher" elements in our nature, but on the shattering and rebuilding, the death and re-birth, of that nature in every part: neither Greek nor Jew nor barbarian, but a new creation.

[Note: *The debate between Lewis and Professor Price did not end here. In* The Socratic Digest, *No. 4 [1948], there follows a "Reply" to Lewis's "Religion without Dogma?" by Professor Price (pp. 94–102). Then, at a meeting of the Socratic Club on 2nd February 1948, Miss G.E.M. Anscombe read a paper entitled "A reply to Mr C.S. Lewis's*

Argument that 'Naturalism is Self-refuting'", *afterwards published in the same issue of the* Digest *(pp. 7–15) as Professor Price's "Reply". Miss Anscombe criticized the argument found on pp. 92–5 of the paper printed above as well as Chapter III, "The Self-Contradiction of the Naturalist", of Lewis's book* Miracles *(London, 1947). The two short pieces that follow are (A) the Socratic minute-book account of Lewis's reply to Miss Anscombe, and (B) a reply written by Lewis himself – both reprinted from the same issue of the* Digest *mentioned above (pp. 15–16). Aware that the third chapter of his* Miracles *was ambiguous, Lewis revised this chapter for the Fontana (1960) issue of* Miracles *in which Chapter III is retitled "The Cardinal Difficulty of Naturalism".*]

A

In his reply Mr C.S. Lewis agreed that the words "cause" and "ground" were far from synonymous but said that the recognition of a ground could be the cause of assent, and that assent was only rational when such was its cause. He denied that such words as "recognition" and "perception" could be properly used of a mental act among whose causes the thing perceived or recognized was not one.

Miss Anscombe said that Mr Lewis had misunderstood her, and thus the first part of the discussion was confined to the two speakers who attempted to clarify their positions and their differences. Miss Anscombe said that Mr Lewis was still not distinguishing between "having reasons" and "having reasoned" in the causal sense. Mr Lewis understood the speaker to be making a tetrachotomy thus: (1) logical reasons; (2) having reasons (i.e. psychological); (3) historical causes; (4) scientific causes or observed regularities. The main point in his reply was that an observed regularity was only the symptom of a cause, and not the cause itself, and in reply to an interruption by the Secretary he referred to his notion of cause as "magical". An open discussion followed, in which some members tried to show Miss Anscombe that there was a connection between ground and cause, while others contended against the President [Lewis] that the test for the validity of reason could never in any event be such a thing as the state of the blood stream. The President finally admitted that the word "valid" was an unfortunate one. From the discussion in general it appeared that Mr Lewis would have to turn his argument into a rigorous analytic one, if his notion of "validity" as the effect of causes were to stand the test of all the questions put to him.

B

I admit that *valid* was a bad word for what I meant; *veridical* (or *verific* or *veriferous*) would have been better. I also admit that the cause and effect relation between events and the ground and consequent relations between propositions are distinct. Since English uses the word *because* of both, let us here use *Because* CE for the cause and effect relation ("This doll always falls on its feet *because* CE its feet are weighted"), and *Because* GC for the ground and consequent relation ("A equals C *because* GC they both equal B"). But the sharper this distinction becomes the more my difficulty increases. If an argument is to be verific the conclusion must be related to the premises as consequent to ground, i.e. the conclusion is there *because* GC certain other propositions are true. On the other hand, our thinking the conclusion is an event and must be related to previous events as effect to cause, i.e. this act of thinking must occur *because* CE previous events have occurred. It would seem, therefore, that we never think the conclusion *because* GC it is the consequent of its grounds but only *because* CE certain previous events have happened. If so, it does not seem that the GC sequence makes us more likely to think the true conclusion than not. And this is very much what I meant by the difficulty in Naturalism.

7

Is Theism Important?[1]

(1952)

I have lost the notes of what I originally said in replying to Professor Price's paper and cannot now remember what it was, except that I welcomed most cordially his sympathy with the Polytheists. I still do. When grave persons express their fear that England is relapsing into Paganism, I am tempted to reply, "Would that she were!" For I do not think it at all likely that we shall ever see Parliament opened by the slaughtering of a garlanded white bull in the House of Lords, or Cabinet Ministers leaving sandwiches in Hyde Park as an offering for the Dryads. If such a state of affairs came about, then the Christian apologist would have something to work on. For a Pagan, as history shows, is a man eminently convertible to Christianity. He is essentially, the pre-Christian, or sub-Christian, religious man. The post-Christian man of our own day differs from him as much as a *divorcée* differs from a virgin. The Christian and the Pagan have much more in common with one another than either has with the writers of the *New Statesman*; and those writers would of course agree with me. For the rest, what now occurs to me after re-reading Professor Price's paper is something like this.

1. I think we must introduce into the discussion a distinction between two senses of the word *Faith*. This may mean (*a*) a settled intellectual assent. In that sense faith (or "belief") in God hardly differs from faith in the uniformity

[1] This is a reply to a paper Professor H.H. Price read to the Oxford Socratic Club. Professor Price's paper was published under the same title in *The Socratic Digest*, No. 5 (1952), pp. 39–47, and Lewis's answer, printed here, was originally published in the same periodical

of nature or in the consciousness of other people. This is what, I think, has sometimes been called a "notional" or "intellectual" or "carnal" faith. It may also mean (*b*) a trust, or confidence, in the God whose existence is thus assented to. This involves an attitude of the will. It is more like our confidence in a friend. It would be generally agreed that Faith in sense A is not a religious state. The devils who "believe and tremble"[1] have Faith-A. A man who curses or ignores God may have Faith-A. Philosophical arguments for the existence of God are presumably intended to produce Faith-A. No doubt those who construct them are anxious to produce Faith-A because it is a necessary precondition of Faith-B, and in that sense their ultimate intention is religious. But their immediate object, the conclusion they attempt to prove, is not. I therefore think they cannot be justly accused of trying to get a religious conclusion out of non-religious premises. I agree with Professor Price that this cannot be done: but I deny that the religious philosophers are trying to do it.

I also think that in some ages, what claim to be Proofs of Theism have had much more efficacy in producing Faith-A than Professor Price suggests. Nearly everyone I know who has embraced Christianity in adult life has been influenced by what seemed to him to be at least probable arguments for Theism. I have known some who were completely convinced by Descartes' Ontological Proof:[2] that is, they received Faith-A from Descartes first and then went on to seek, and to find, Faith-B. Even quite uneducated people who have been Christians all their lives not infrequently appeal to some simplified form of the Argument from Design. Even acceptance of tradition implies an argument which sometimes becomes explicit in the form "I reckon all

[1] James 2:19
[2] This is briefly summed up in René Descartes' *Discours de la Méthode*, Part iv, in which he says "I think, therefore I am"

those wise men wouldn't have believed in it if it weren't true."

Of course Faith-A usually involves a degree of subjective certitude which goes beyond the logical certainty, or even the supposed logical certainty, of the arguments employed. It may retain this certitude for a long time, I expect, even without the support of Faith-B. This excess of certitude in a settled assent is not at all uncommon. Most of those who believe in Uniformity of Nature, Evolution, or the Solar System, share it.

2. I doubt whether religious people have ever supposed that Faith-B follows automatically on the acquisition of Faith-A. It is described as a "gift".[1] As soon as we have Faith-A in the existence of God, we are instructed to ask from God Himself the gift of Faith-B. An odd request, you may say, to address to a First Cause, an *Ens Realissimum*, or an *Unmoved Mover*. It might be argued, and I think I would argue myself, that even such an aridly philosophical God rather fails to invite than actually repels a personal approach. It would, at any rate, do no harm to try it. But I fully admit that most of those who, having reached Faith-A, pray for Faith-B, do so because they have already had something like religious experience. Perhaps the best way of putting it would be to say that Faith-A converts into religious experience what was hitherto only potentially or implicitly religious. In this modified form I would accept Professor Price's view that philosophical proofs never, by themselves, lead to religion. Something at least *quasi*-religious uses them before, and the "proofs" remove an inhibition which was preventing their development into religion proper.

This is not exactly *fides quaerens intellectum*,[2] for these quasi-religious experiences were not *fides*. In spite of Pro-

[1] e.g. 1 Corinthians 12: 1–11; Ephesians 2:8
[2] faith seeking understanding

fessor Price's rejection I still think Otto's account of the Numinous[1] is the best analysis of them we have. I believe it is a mistake to regard the Numinous as merely an affair of "feeling". Admittedly, Otto can describe it only by referring to the emotions it arouses in us; but then nothing can be described except in terms of its effects in consciousness. We have in English an exact name for the emotion aroused by the Numinous, which Otto, writing in German, lacked; we have the word Awe — an emotion very like fear, with the important difference that it need imply no estimate of danger. When we fear a tiger, we fear that it may kill us: when we fear a ghost — well, we just fear the ghost, not this or that mischief which it may do us. The Numinous or Awful is that of which we have this, as it were, objectless or disinterested fear — this awe. And "the Numinous" is not a name for our own feeling of Awe any more than "the Contemptible" is a name for contempt. It is the answer to the question "Of what do you feel awe?" And what we feel awe of is certainly not itself awe.

With Otto and, in a sense, with Professor Price, I would find the seed of religious experience in our experience of the Numinous. In an age like our own such experience does occur but, until religion comes and retrospectively transforms it, it usually appears to the subject to be a special form of aesthetic experience. In ancient times I think experience of the Numinous developed into the Holy only in so far as the Numinous (not in itself at all necessarily moral) came to be connected with the morally good. This happened regularly in Israel, sporadically elsewhere. But even in the higher Paganism, I do not think this process led to anything exactly like *fides*. There is nothing credal in Paganism. In Israel we do get *fides* but this is always connected with certain historical affirmations. Faith is not simply in the numinous *Elohim*, nor even simply in the holy Jahweh, but in the God "of our

[1] Rudolf Otto, *The Idea of the Holy*, trans. John W. Harvey (London, 1923)

fathers", the God who called Abraham and brought Israel out of Egypt. In Christianity this historical element is strongly re-affirmed. The object of faith is at once the *ens entium*[1] of the philosophers, the Awful Mystery of Paganism, the Holy Law given of the moralists, and Jesus of Nazareth who was crucified under Pontius Pilate and rose again on the third day.

Thus we must admit that Faith, as we know it, does not flow from philosophical argument alone; nor from experience of the Numinous alone; nor from moral experience alone; nor from history alone; but from historical events which at once fulfil and transcend the moral category, which link themselves with the most numinous elements in Paganism, and which (as it seems to us) demand as their presupposition the existence of a Being who is more, but not less, than the God whom many reputable philosophers think they can establish.

Religious experience, as we know it, really involves all these elements. We may, however, use the word in a narrower sense to denote moments of mystical, or devotional, or merely numinous experience; and we may then ask, with Professor Price, how such moments, being a kind of *visio*, are related to faith, which by definition is "not sight". This does not seem to me one of the hardest questions. "Religious experience" in the narrower sense comes and goes: especially goes. The operation of Faith is to retain, so far as the will and intellect are concerned, what is irresistible and obvious during the moments of special grace. By faith we believe always what we hope hereafter to see always and perfectly and have already seen imperfectly and by flashes. In relation to the philosophical premises a Christian's faith is of course excessive: in relation to what is sometimes shown him, it is perhaps just as often defective. My faith even in an earthly friend goes beyond all that could be demonstratively proved; yet in another sense I may often trust him less than he deserves.

---

[1] being of beings

8

Rejoinder to Dr Pittenger[1]

(1958)

To one of the charges Dr Norman Pittenger makes in his
"Critique" in the 1st October *Christian Century*,[1] I must
with shame plead guilty. He has caught me using the word
"literally" where I did not really mean it, a vile journalistic
cliché which he cannot reprobate more severely than I now
do myself.[2]

I must also admit some truth in his charge of
Apollinarianism; there is a passage in my *Problem of Pain*
which would imply, if pressed, a shockingly crude conception of the Incarnation. I corrected it by a footnote to
the French edition but have not been able to do so
elsewhere, save in so far as *Mere Christianity*, Book Four,
chapter three, may provide an antidote.

This must not be taken to mean that my present conception would fully satisfy Dr Pittenger. He speaks about
"the validity of our Lord's unique place in Christian faith
as that One in whom God was so active and so present that
he may be called 'God-Man'".[3] I am not quite sure what
this means. May I translate it, "Our Lord's actually unique
place in the structure of utter reality, the unique mode, as

---

[1] W. Norman Pittenger. "A Critique of C.S. Lewis", *Christian Century*,
Vol. LXXV (1st October 1958), pp. 1104–7

[2] In *Broadcast Talks* (London, 1942), Part II, ch. 5, p. 60, Lewis had
written that "the whole mass of Christians are literally the physical
organism through which Christ acts – that we are His fingers and
muscles, the cells of His body." The word "literally", however, was
deleted when *Broadcast Talks* was reprinted with two other short
books as *Mere Christianity* (London, 1952) in which the phrase quoted
above is found in Bk. II, ch. 5, p. 51

[3] Pittenger, p. 1106

well as degree, of God's presence and action in Him, make the formula 'God-Man' the objectively true description of Him"? If so, I think we are very nearly agreed. Or must I translate it, "the unique place which Christians (subjectively, in their own thoughts) gave to our Lord as One in whom God was present and active to a unique degree made it reasonable for them to call Him God-Man"? If so, I must demur. In other words, if Dr Pittenger's "may be called" means anything less or other than "is", I could not accept his formula. For I think that Jesus Christ is (in fact) the only Son of God – that is, the only original Son of God, through whom others are enabled to "become sons of God".[1] If Dr Pittenger wishes to attack that doctrine, I wonder he should choose me as its representative. It has had champions far worthier of his steel.

I turn next to my book *Miracles* and am sorry to say that I here have to meet Dr Pittenger's charges with straight denials. He says that this book "opens with a definition of miracles as the 'violation' of the laws of nature".[2] He is mistaken. The passage (chapter 2) really runs: "I use the word *Miracle* to mean an interference with Nature by supernatural power."[3] If Dr Pittenger thinks the difference between the true text and his mis-quotation merely verbal, he has misunderstood nearly the whole book. I never equated nature (the spatio-temporal system of facts and events) with the laws of nature (the patterns into which these facts and events fall). I would as soon equate an actual speech with the rules of grammar. In chapter eight I say in so many words that no miracle either can or need break the laws of nature; that "it is . . . inaccurate to define

---

[1] John 1:12
[2] Pittenger, p. 1105
[3] *Miracles: A Preliminary Study* (London, 1947). Because Lewis later revised chapter III of this book, all my text-references are to the "revised" paperback edition of *Miracles* (Fontana Books, London, 1960), p. 9

a miracle as something that breaks the laws of Nature";[1] and that "The divine art of miracle is not an art of suspending the pattern to which events conform but of feeding new events into that pattern."[2] How many times does a man need to say something before he is safe from the accusation of having said exactly the opposite? (I am not for a moment imputing dishonesty to Dr Pittenger; we all know too well how difficult it is to grasp or retain the substance of a book one finds antipathetic.)

Again, Dr Pittenger contrasts my view with that which makes miracles a sign of God's action and presence in creation. Yet in chapter fifteen I say that the miracle at Cana manifests "the God of Israel who has through all these centuries given us wine", and that in the miraculous feedings God "does close and small . . . what He has always been doing in the seas, the lakes and the little brooks".[3] Surely this is just what Dr Pittenger wanted me to say, and what Athanasius says (*De Incarnatione* xiv. 8, edited by F.L. Cross, 1939)?

It is very true that I make no use of the different words (*semeia, terata* and the rest) which New Testament writers use for miracles. But why should I? I was writing for people who wanted to know whether the things could have happened rather than what they should be called; whether we could without absurdity believe that Christ rose from the emptied tomb. I am afraid most of my readers, if once convinced that He did not, would have felt it of minor importance to decide whether, if He had done so, this nonexistent event would have been a *teras* or a *dunamis*. And (in certain moods) one does, after all, see their point.

Dr Pittenger thinks the Naturalist whom I try to refute in chapter three is a man of straw. He may not be found in the

[1] ibid., p. 63
[2] ibid., p. 64
[3] ibid., pp. 140, 141

circles Dr Pittenger frequents. He is quite common where I come from; and, presumably, in Moscow. There is indeed a really serious hitch in that chapter (which ought to be rewritten) but Dr Pittenger has not seen it or has charitably kept silent about it.[1]

I now turn to the more difficult and interesting question of the Fourth Gospel. It is difficult because, here again, I do not quite understand what Dr Pittenger writes. He blames me for putting all four gospels in the same category, and especially for believing that Jesus claimed deity because the Fourth Gospel says He did. But this does not mean that Dr Pittenger rejects the fourth as simply untrue. According to him it gives that "interpretation" of Our Lord's "significance" which the early Christians "found", and "rightly" found, "to be true".[2] Now in my language that significance of anything which is "rightly found to be true" would be its true significance and those who found it would have found what the thing really meant. If the Fourth Gospel gives us what Jesus Christ really meant, why am I blamed for accepting it? But I am, and therefore Dr Pittenger's words must bear some other sense. Does he mean that what they "rightly found to be true" was not true? Or that the significance which was rightly found to be true by them would be "wrongly found" to be true by us? Or did they get the "significance" right and go wrong about the "interpretation of the significance"? I give it up.

I confess, however, that the problem of the Fourth Gospel raises in me a conflict between authority and private judgement: the authority of all those learned men who think that Gospel unhistorical, and my judgement as a literary critic which constrains me to think it at least as close to the facts as Boswell's *Johnson*. If I venture here to

[1] Lewis did, as just mentioned in a footnote above, revise chapter III of *Miracles*
[2] Pittenger, p. 1106

follow judgement in the teeth of authority, this is partly because I could never see how one escaped the dilemma *aut deus aut malus homo*[1] by confining oneself to the Synoptics. Moderns do not seem startled, as contemporaries were, by the claim Jesus there makes to forgive sins; not sins against Himself, just sins. Yet surely, if they actually met it, they would feel differently. If Dr Pittenger told me that two of his colleagues had lost him a professorship by telling lies about his character and I replied, "I freely forgive them both", would he not think this an impertinence (both in the old and in the modern sense) bordering on insanity? And of course all three Synoptics tell the story of One who, at His trial, sealed His fate by saying he was the Son of God.

I am accused of attributing "almost spatial transcendence" to God and of denying His continued presence within nature because I speak of Him as "invading" or "intruding into" her.[2] This is really very hard of the Doctor. Of course the very word "transcendence" contains a spatial image. So does "immanence". So does Dr Pittenger's "God's action and *presence in* the creation".[3] We must, after all, speak the language of men. (I have got much light on this problem from Edwyn Bevan's *Symbolism and Belief*.) But I freely admit that, believing both, I have stressed the transcendence of God more than His immanence. I thought, and think, that the present situation demands this. I see around me no danger of Deism but much of an immoral, naïve and sentimental pantheism. I have often found that it was in fact the chief obstacle to conversion.

Dr Pittenger says that I base the Faith on authority (which has "grown up in the Church and won the assent of

[1] Either God or a bad man
[2] Pittenger, p. 1105
[3] ibid.

great doctors").[1] So does he; his authority is "the total consentient witness of all Christians from the apostles' time".[2] I am not sure why he calls my authority "mechanical". Surely it differs from his mainly by being discoverable? The "total consentient witness" would be grand if we had it. But of course the overwhelming majority of Christians, as of other men, have died, and are dying while I write, without recording their "witness". How does Dr Pittenger consult his authority?

Where he really hurt me was in the charge of callousness to animals. Surprised me too; for the very same passage is blamed by others for extreme sentimentality.[3] It is hard to please all. But if the Patagonians think me a dwarf and the Pygmies a giant, perhaps my stature is in fact fairly unremarkable.

The statement that I do not "care much for" the Sermon on the Mount but "prefer" the "Pauline ethic" of man's sinfulness and helplessness[4] carries a suggestion of alternatives between which we may choose, where I see successive stages through which we must proceed. Most of my books are evangelistic, addressed to *tous exo*. It would have been inept to preach forgiveness and a Saviour to those who did not know they were in need of either. Hence St Paul's and the Baptist's diagnosis (would you call it exactly an *ethic*?) had to be pressed. Nor am I aware that Our Lord revised it ("if ye, being evil . . .").[5] As to "caring for" the Sermon on the Mount, if "caring for" here means "liking" or enjoying, I suppose no one "cares for" it. Who can *like* being knocked flat on his face by a sledge-

[1] Pittenger, p. 1106, quoting Lewis's *Problem of Pain* (London, 1940), ch. v, p. 60
[2] Pittenger, p. 1106
[3] The reference is to the chapter on "Animal Pain" in *The Problem of Pain*.
[4] Pittenger, p. 1106
[5] Matthew 7:11; Luke 11:13

hammer? I can hardly imagine a more deadly spiritual condition than that of the man who can read that passage with
tranquil pleasure. This is indeed to be "at ease in Zion".[1]
Such a man is not yet ripe for the Bible; he had better start by
learning sense from Islam: "The Heaven and the Earth and
all between, thinkest thou I made them *in jest?*"

And this illustrates what appears to me to be a weakness
in the Doctor's critical method. He judges my books *in
vacuo*, with no consideration of the audience to whom they
were addressed or the prevalent errors they were trying to
combat. The Naturalist becomes a straw man because he is
not found among "first-rate scientists" and readers of
Einstein. But I was writing *ad populum*, not *ad clerum*.
This is relevant to my manner as well as my matter. It is
true, I do not understand why it is vulgar or offensive, in
speaking of the Holy Trinity, to illustrate from plane and
solid geometry the conception that what is self-
contradictory on one level may be consistent on another.[2] I
could have understood the Doctor's being shocked if I had
compared God to an unjust judge, or Christ to a thief in the
night; but mathematical objects seem to me as free from
sordid associations as any the mind can entertain.

But let all that pass. Suppose the image is vulgar. If it gets
across to the unbeliever what the unbeliever desperately
needs to know, the vulgarity must be endured. Indeed, the
image's very vulgarity may be an advantage; for there is
much sense in the reasons advanced by Aquinas (following
Pseudo-Dionysius) for preferring to present divine truths
sub figuris vilium corporum[3] (*Summa Theologica*, Qu. 1,
Art. 9 *ad tertium*).

[1] Amos 6:1
[2] In *Mere Christianity*, Bk. iv, ch. 2, p. 128, Lewis says "In God's
dimension, so to speak, you find a being who is three Persons while
remaining one Being, just as a cube is six squares while remaining one
cube"
[3] under the figure of vile bodies

When I began, Christianity came before the great mass of my unbelieving fellow countrymen either in the highly emotional form offered by revivalists or in the unintelligible language of highly cultured clergymen. Most men were reached by neither. My task was therefore simply that of a *translator* – one turning Christian doctrine, or what he believed to be such, into the vernacular, into language that unscholarly people would attend to and could understand. For this purpose a style more guarded, more *nuancé*, finelier shaded, more rich in fruitful ambiguities – in fact, a style more like Dr Pittinger's own – would have been worse than useless. It would not only have failed to enlighten the common reader's understanding; it would have aroused suspicion. He would have thought, poor soul, that I was facing both ways, sitting on the fence, offering at one moment what I withdrew the next, and generally trying to trick him. I may have made theological errors. My manner may have been defective. Others may do better hereafter. I am ready, if I am young enough, to learn. Dr Pittenger would be a more helpful critic if he advised a cure as well as asserting many diseases. How does he himself do such work? What methods, and with what success, does he employ when he is trying to convert the great mass of storekeepers, lawyers, realtors, morticians, policemen and artisans who surround him in his own city?

One thing at least is sure. If the real theologians had tackled this laborious work of translation about a hundred years ago, when they began to lose touch with the people (for whom Christ died), there would have been no place for me.[1]

[1] See Letter 11, p. 141

9

Willing Slaves of the Welfare State[1]
(1958)

Progress means movement in a desired direction, and we do not all desire the same things for our species. In "Possible Worlds"[2] Professor Haldane pictured a future in which Man, foreseeing that Earth would soon be uninhabitable, adapted himself for migration to Venus by drastically modifying his physiology and abandoning justice, pity and happiness. The desire here is for mere survival. Now I care far more *how* humanity lives than how long. Progress, for me, means increasing goodness and happiness of individual lives. For the species, as for each man, mere longevity seems to me a contemptible ideal.

I therefore go even further than C.P. Snow in removing the H-bomb from the centre of the picture. Like him, I am not certain whether if it killed one-third of us (the one-third I belong to), this would be a bad thing for the remainder; like him, I don't think it will kill us all. But suppose it did? As a Christian I take it for granted that human history will some day end; and I am offering Omniscience no

---

[1] From the French Revolution to the outbreak of the First World War in 1914, it was generally assumed that progress in human affairs was not only possible but inevitable. Since then two terrible wars and the discovery of the hydrogen bomb have made men question this confident assumption. *The Observer* invited five well-known writers to give their answers to the following questions: "Is man progressing today?" "Is progress even possible?" This second article in the series is a reply to the opening article by C.P. Snow, "Man in Society", *The Observer* (13th July, 1958)

[2] One essay in J.B.S. Haldane's *Possible Worlds and Other Essays* (London, 1927). See also "The Last Judgement" in the same book

advice as to the best date for that consummation. I am more concerned by what the Bomb is doing already.

One meets young people who make the threat of it a reason for poisoning every pleasure and evading every duty in the present. Didn't they know that, Bomb or no Bomb, all men die (many in horrible ways)? There is no good moping and sulking about it.

Having removed what I think a red herring, I return to the real question. Are people becoming, or likely to become, better or happier? Obviously this allows only the most conjectural answer. Most individual experience (and there is no other kind) never gets into the news, let alone the history books; one has an imperfect grasp even of one's own. We are reduced to generalities. Even among these it is hard to strike a balance. Sir Charles enumerates many real ameliorations. Against these we must set Hiroshima, Black and Tans, Gestapo, Ogpu, brain-washing, the Russian slave camps. Perhaps we grow kinder to children; but then we grow less kind to the old. Any GP will tell you that even prosperous people refuse to look after their parents. "Can't they be got into some sort of Home?" says Goneril.[1]

More useful, I think, than an attempt at balancing, is the reminder that most of these phenomena, good and bad, are made possible by two things. These two will probably determine most of what happens to us for some time.

The first is the advance, and increasing application, of science. As a means to the ends I care for, this is neutral. We shall grow able to cure, and to produce, more diseases – bacterial war, not bombs, might ring down the curtain – to alleviate, and to inflict, more pains, to husband, or to waste, the resources of the planet more extensively. We can become either more beneficent or more mischievous. My guess is that we shall do both; mending one thing and marring another, removing old miseries and producing

[1] In Shakespeare's *King Lear*

119

new ones, safeguarding ourselves here and endangering ourselves there.

The second is the changed relation between Government and subjects. Sir Charles mentions our new attitude to crime. I will mention the trainloads of Jews delivered at the German gas-chambers. It seems shocking to suggest a common element, but I think one exists. On the humanitarian view all crime is pathological; it demands not retributive punishment but cure. This separates the criminal's treatment from the concepts of justice and desert; a "just cure" is meaningless.

On the old view public opinion might protest against a punishment (it protested against our old penal code) as excessive, more than the man "deserved"; an ethical question on which anyone might have an opinion. But a remedial treatment can be judged only by the probability of its success; a technical question on which only experts can speak. Thus the criminal ceases to be a person, a subject of rights and duties, and becomes merely an object on which society can work. And this is, in principle, how Hitler treated the Jews. They were objects; killed not for ill desert but because, on his theories, they were a disease in society. If society can mend, remake and unmake men at its pleasure, its pleasure may, of course, be humane or homicidal. The difference is important. But, either way, rulers have become owners.

Observe how the "humane" attitude to crime could operate. If crimes are diseases, why should diseases be treated differently from crimes? And who but the experts can define disease? One school of psychology regards my religion as a neurosis. If this neurosis ever becomes inconvenient to Government, what is to prevent my being subjected to a compulsory "cure"? It may be painful; treatments sometimes are. But it will be no use asking, "What have I done to deserve this?" The Straightener will reply:

"But, my dear fellow, no one's *blaming* you. We no longer believe in retributive justice. We're healing you."

This would be no more than an extreme application of the political philosophy implicit in most modern communities. It has stolen on us unawares. Two wars necessitated vast curtailments of liberty, and we have grown, though grumblingly, accustomed to our chains. The increasing complexity and precariousness of our economic life have forced Government to take over many spheres of activity once left to choice or chance. Our intellectuals have surrendered first to the slave-philosophy of Hegel, then to Marx, finally to the linguistic analysts.

As a result, classical political theory, with its Stoical, Christian and juristic key-conceptions (natural law, the value of the individual, the rights of man), has died. The modern State exists not to protect our rights but to do us good or make us good — anyway, to do something to us or to make us something. Hence the new name "leaders" for those who were once "rulers". We are less their subjects than their wards, pupils, or domestic animals. There is nothing left of which we can say to them, "Mind your own business." Our whole lives *are* their business.

I write "they" because it seems childish not to recognize that actual government is and always must be oligarchical. Our effective masters must be more than one and fewer than all. But the oligarchs begin to regard us in a new way.

Here, I think, lies our real dilemma. Probably we cannot, certainly we shall not, retrace our steps. We are tamed animals (some with kind, some with cruel, masters) and should probably starve if we got out of our cage. That is one horn of the dilemma. But in an increasingly planned society, how much of what I value can survive? That is the other horn.

I believe a man is happier, and happy in a richer way, if he has "the freeborn mind". But I doubt whether he can have this without economic independence, which the new society is abolishing. For economic independence allows an education not controlled by Government; and in adult life it is the man who needs, and asks, nothing of the Government who can criticize its acts and snap his fingers at its ideology. Read Montaigne; that's the voice of a man with his legs under his own table, eating the mutton and turnips raised on his own land. Who will talk like that when the State is everyone's schoolmaster and employer? Admittedly, when man was untamed, such liberty belonged only to the few. I know. Hence the horrible suspicion that our only choice is between societies with few freemen and societies with none.

Again, the new oligarchy must more and more base its claim to plan us on its claim to knowledge. If we are to be mothered, mother must know best. This means they must increasingly rely on the advice of scientists, till in the end the politicians proper become merely the scientists' puppets. Technocracy is the form to which planned society must tend. Now I dread specialists in power because they are specialists speaking outside their special subjects. Let scientists tell us about sciences. But government involves questions about the good for man, and justice, and what things are worth having at what price; and on these a scientific training gives a man's opinion no added value. Let the doctor tell me I shall die unless I do so-and-so; but whether life is worth having on those terms is no more a question for him than for any other man.

Thirdly, I do not like the pretensions of Government – the grounds on which it demands my obedience – to be pitched too high. I don't like the medicine man's magical pretensions nor the Bourbon's Divine Right. This is not solely because I disbelieve in magic and in Bossuet's *Politique*.[1] I believe in God, but I detest theocracy. For every

[1] Jacques Bénigne Bossuet, *Politique tirée des propres paroles de l'Écriture-Sainte* (Paris, 1709)

Government consists of mere men and is, strictly viewed, a makeshift; if it adds to its commands "Thus saith the Lord", it lies, and lies dangerously.

On just the same ground I dread government in the name of science. That is how tyrannies come in. In every age the men who want us under their thumb, if they have any sense, will put forward the particular pretension which the hopes and fears of that age render most potent. They "cash in". It has been magic, it has been Christianity. Now it will certainly be science. Perhaps the real scientists may not think much of the tyrants' "science" – they didn't think much of Hitler's racial theories or Stalin's biology. But they can be muzzled.

We must give full weight to Sir Charles's reminder that millions in the East are still half starved. To these my fears would seem very unimportant. A hungry man thinks about food, not freedom. We must give full weight to the claim that nothing but science, and science globally applied, and therefore unprecedented Government controls, can produce full bellies and medical care for the whole human race: nothing, in short, but a world Welfare State. It is a full admission of these truths which impresses upon me the extreme peril of humanity at present.

We have on the one hand a desperate need: hunger, sickness and the dread of war. We have, on the other, the conception of something that might meet it: omnicompetent global technocracy. Are not these the ideal opportunity for enslavement? This is how it has entered before: a desperate need (real or apparent) in the one party, a power (real or apparent) to relieve it, in the other. In the ancient world individuals have sold themselves as slaves, in order to eat. So in society. Here is a witch-doctor who can save us from the sorcerers – a war-lord who can save us from the barbarians – a Church that can save us from Hell. Give them what they ask, give ourselves to them bound and blindfold, if only they will! Perhaps the terrible bargain will be made again. We cannot blame men for making it. We can hardly wish them not to. Yet we can hardly bear that they should.

The question about progress has become the question whether we can discover any way of submitting to the world-wide paternalism of a technocracy without losing all the personal privacy and independence. Is there any possibility of getting the super Welfare State's honey and avoiding the sting?

Let us make no mistake about the sting. The Swedish sadness is only a foretaste. To live his life in his own way, to call his house his castle, to enjoy the fruits of his own labour, to educate his children as his conscience directs, to save for their prosperity after his death – these are wishes deeply ingrained in white and civilized man. Their realization is almost as necessary to our virtues as to our happiness. From their total frustration disastrous results, both moral and psychological, might follow.

All this threatens us even if the form of society which our needs point to should prove an unparalleled success. But is that certain? What assurance have we that our masters will or can keep the promise which induced us to sell ourselves? Let us not be deceived by phrases about "Man taking charge of his own destiny". All that can really happen is that some men will take charge of the destiny of the others. They will be simply men; none perfect; some greedy, cruel and dishonest. The more completely we are planned the more powerful they will be. Have we discovered some new reason why, this time, power should not corrupt as it has done before?

10

Letters

[Though I have reprinted only Lewis's own letters here, I have attempted to place them in their proper contexts by citing the sources of the letters from the various correspondents which Lewis was answering, or who were answering him. Thus the sub-divisions (a), (b), (c), and so forth. – Ed.]

1

The Conditions for a Just War

(a) E.L. Mascall, "The Christian and the Next War", *Theology*, Vol. XXXVIII (January 1939), pp. 53–8

(b) C.S. Lewis, "The Conditions for a Just War", ibid. (May 1939), pp. 373–4

Sir,

In your January number Mr Mascall mentions six conditions for a just war which have been laid down by "theologians". I have one question to ask, and a number of problems to raise, about these rules. The question is merely historical. Who are these theologians, and what kind or degree of authority can they claim over members of the Church of England? The problems are more difficult. Condition 4 lays down that "it must be morally certain that the losses, to the belligerents, the world, and religion, will not outweigh the advantages of winning"; and 6, that "there must be a considerable probability of winning". It is plain that equally sincere people can differ to any extent and argue for ever as to whether a proposed war fulfils these conditions or not. The practical question, therefore, which faces us is one of authority. Who has the duty of deciding when the conditions are fulfilled, and the right of enforcing his decision? Modern discussions tend to assume without argument that the answer is "The private conscience of the individual", and that any other answer is immoral and totalitarian. Now it is certain, in some sense, that "no duty of obedience can justify a sin", as Mr Mascall says. Granted that capital punishment is compatible with Christianity, a Christian may lawfully be a hangman; but he must not hang a man whom he knows to be innocent. But will anyone interpret this to mean that the hangman has the *same* duty of investigating the prisoner's guilt which the judge has? If so, no executive can work and no Christian state is possible; which is absurd. I conclude that the hangman has done his duty if he has done his share of the general duty, resting upon all citizens alike, to ensure, so far as in him lies, that we have an honest judicial system; if, in spite of this, and unknowingly, he hangs an innocent man, then a sin has been committed, but not by him. This analogy suggests to me that it must be absurd to give to the private citizen the *same* right and duty of deciding the justice of a given war which rests on governments; and I submit that the rules for determining what wars are just were originally rules for the guidance of princes, not subjects. This does not mean that private persons must obey governments commanding them to do what they know is sin; but perhaps it does mean (I write it with some reluctance) that the ultimate decision as to what the situation at a given moment is in the highly complex field of international affairs is one which must be delegated. No doubt we must make every effort which the constitution allows to ensure a good government and to influence public opinion;

but in the long run, the nation, as a nation, must act, and it can act only through its government. (It must be remembered that there are risks in both directions: if war is ever lawful, then peace is sometimes sinful.) What is the alternative? That individuals ignorant of history and strategy should decide for themselves whether condition 6 ("a considerable probability of winning") is, or is not, fulfilled? – or that every citizen, neglecting his own vocation and not weighing his capacity, is to become an expert on all the relevant, and often technical, problems?

Decisions by the private conscience of each Christian in the light of Mr Mascall's six rules would divide Christians from each other and result in no clear Christian witness to the pagan world around us. But a clear Christian witness might be attained in a different way. If all Christians consented to bear arms at the command of the magistrate, and if all, after that, refused to obey anti-Christian orders, should we not get a clear issue? A man is much more certain that he ought not to murder prisoners or bomb civilians than he ever can be about the justice of a war. It is perhaps here that "conscientious objection" ought to begin. I feel certain that one Christian airman shot for refusing to bomb enemy civilians would be a more effective martyr (in the etymological sense of the word) than a hundred Christians in jail for refusing to join the army.

Christendom has made two efforts to deal with the evil of war – chivalry and pacifism. Neither succeeded. But I doubt whether chivalry has such an unbroken record of failure as pacifism.

The question is a very dark one. I should welcome about equally refutation, or development, of what I have said.

2

The Conflict in Anglican Theology

(a) Oliver C. Quick, "The Conflict in Anglican Theology", *Theology*, Vol. LXI (October 1940), pp. 234–7

(b) C.S. Lewis, ibid. (November 1940), p. 304

Sir,

In an admirable letter contributed to your October number Canon Quick remarks, "'Moderns' of every kind have one characteristic in common: they hate Liberalism." Would it not be equally true to say, more shortly, "'Moderns' of every kind have one characteristic in common: they *hate*?" The matter deserves, perhaps, more attention than it has received.

3

Miracles

(a) Peter May, "Miracles", *The Guardian* (9th October 1942), p. 323

(b) C.S. Lewis, ibid. (16th October 1942), p. 331

Sir,

In answer to Mr May's question, I reply that whether the birth of St John Baptist were a miracle or no, it was not the same miracle as the birth of our Lord.[1] What was abnormal about St Elizabeth's pregnancy was that she was an elderly (married) woman, hitherto sterile. That Zacharias was the father of St John is implied in the text ("shall bear *thee* a son", Luke 1:13).

[1] Mr May was criticizing Lewis's essay on "Miracles" in *God in the Dock*

Of the natural conversion of water into wine, what I said was: "God creates the vine and teaches it to draw up water by its roots and, *with the aid of the sun*, to turn that water into a juice *which will ferment* and take on certain qualities."[1] For completeness I should, no doubt, have added "with the aid of the soil", and perhaps other things; but this would not, from my point of view, have materially altered what I was saying. My answer to Mr May's question – where the other raw materials came from – would be the same, whether the list of raw materials be reduced to the mere vegetable and sunlight I mentioned, or extended to bring in all that the skilled botanist might add. I think they came from the same source at Cana whence they come in nature. I agree with Mr May, of course, that on the hypothesis of the story being fiction, we can attach to it, as our ancestors did to the miracles in Ovid, any number of edifying *moralitates*. What I was doing was to combat that particular argument for its falsity which rests on the idea that, if it occurred, such an event would be arbitrary and meaningless.

4

Mr C.S. Lewis on Christianity

(a) W.R. Childe, "Mr C.S. Lewis on Christianity", *The Listener*, Vol. XXXI (2nd March 1944), p. 245

(b) C.S. Lewis, ibid. (9th March 1944), p. 273

I agree with Mr W.R. Childe that it is no use to say "Lord, Lord", if we do not do what Christ tells us: that, indeed, is one of the reasons why I think an aesthetic religion of

---

[1] *God in the Dock*, p. 16

"flowers and music" insufficient.[1] My reason for thinking that a mere statement of even the highest ethical principles is not enough is precisely that to know these things is not necessarily to do them, and if Christianity brought no healing to the impotent will, Christ's teaching would not help us. I cannot blame Mr Childe for misunderstanding me, because I am naturally no judge of my own lucidity; but I take it very hard that a total stranger whom I have never knowingly injured or offended, on the first discovery of a difference in theological opinion between us, should publicly accuse me of being a potential torturer, murderer and tyrant – for that is what Mr Childe's reference to faggots means if it means anything. How little I approve of compulsion in religion may be gauged from a recent letter of mine to the *Spectator* protesting against the intolerable tyranny of compulsory church parades for the Home Guard. If Mr Childe can find any passage in my works which favours religious or anti-religious compulsion I will give five pounds to any (not militantly anti-Christian) charity he cares to name. If he cannot, I ask him, for justice and charity's sake, to withdraw his charge.

(c) W.R. Childe, ibid. (16th March 1944), p. 301

5

A Village Experience

C.S. Lewis, "A Village Experience", *The Guardian* (31st August 1945), p. 335

[1] Mr Childe had taken exception with a passage in Lewis's BBC broadcast "The Map and the Ocean" in which he said, in speaking of a "vague religion", that "you will not get eternal life by just feeling the presence of God in flowers or music". *The Listener*, Vol. XXXI (24th February 1944), p. 216. The broadcast was later to become a chapter in Lewis's *Mere Christianity* (London, 1952), Bk. IV, ch. i. p. 122

Sir,

I think your readers should, and will, be interested in the following extract from a letter I have just received; the writer is an invalid lady in a village:

"This used to be a God-fearing village with a God- fearing parson who visited and ran the Scouts ('Lovely troop he 'ad. *And* you should have 'eard our choir of a Sunday', says my bricklayer host). The young were polished up and sent to Sunday school, their parents filled the church to the brim. *Now* they have an octogenarian. No harm in that! My late uncle – at that age – was going as strong as most two-year-olds. But this one – I noted for myself, seeing him pass – has been dead for years . . . He does not visit the sick, even if asked. He does nothing. And – listen – he stuck up a notice in the church: *No children admitted without their parents or an adult.* The village . . . went instantly Pagan. I must get away from it. Never before but in the vile pagan West Indies have I been without so much as an *extorted* Holy Sacrament. (*Can* one forbid the church to a Crissom child? – legally, I mean? Pass me a Bishop.)"

6

Correspondence with an Anglican who Dislikes Hymns[1]

(a) Summary of a letter from Erik Routley to Lewis (dated 13th July 1946), p. 15

". . . The Hymn Society of Great Britain and Ireland is opening a file of new hymns to which modern hymn-

---

[1] The "correspondence" consists of two letters from Erik Routley to Lewis and two letters from Lewis, all of which were published together in *The Presbyter*, Vol. VI, No. 2 (1948), pp. 15–20. Lewis's letters were published in *The Presbyter* over the initials "A.B."

writers are to be asked to contribute. I have been asked to write to you and ask if you will be a member of the panel to whom new hymns may be submitted in order that their merit may be assessed . . ."

  (b) C.S. Lewis to Erik Routley (dated 16th July 1946), p. 15

Dear Mr Routley,

  The truth is that I'm not in sufficient sympathy with the project to help you. I know that many of the congregation like singing hymns: but am not yet convinced that their enjoyment is of a spiritual kind. It may be: I don't know. To the minority, of whom I am one, the hymns are mostly the dead wood of the service. Recently in a party of six people I found that all without exception would like *fewer* hymns. Naturally, one holding this view can't help you.

  (c) Erik Routley to Lewis (dated 18th September 1946), pp. 15–20

  (d) C.S. Lewis to Erik Routley (dated 21st September 1946), p. 20

I can't quite remember my own last letter; but I was wrong if I said or implied that (*a*) variables, (*b*) active participation by the people, or (*c*) hymns, were bad in principle. I would agree that anything the congregation *can do* may properly and profitably be offered to God in public worship. If one had a congregation (say, in Africa) who had a high tradition in sacred dancing and could do it really well I would be perfectly in favour of making a dance part of the service. But I wouldn't transfer the practice to a Willesden congregation whose best dance was a ballroom shuffle. In modern England, however, we can't sing – as the Welsh and Germans can. Also (a great pity, but a fact) the art of poetry has developed for two centuries in a private and subjective direction. That is why I find hymns "dead wood". But I spoke only for myself and a few others. If an improved hymnody – or even the present hymnody – does edify other people, of course it is an elementary duty of charity and humility for me to submit. I have never spoken in public *against* the use of hymns: on the contrary I have often told "highbrow" converts that a humble acquiescence in anything that may edify their uneducated brethren (however frightful it seems to the educated "natural man") is the first lesson they must learn. The door is *low* and one must stoop to enter.

7

The Church's Liturgy, Invocation,
and Invocation of Saints

(a) E.L. Mascall, "Quadringentesimo Anno", *Church Times*, Vol. CXXXII (6th May 1949), p. 282

(b) C.S. Lewis, "The Church's Liturgy", ibid. (20th May 1949), p. 319

Sir,

If it is not harking back too far, I would like to make two layman's comments on the liturgical articles in your issue of 6th May. Firstly, I would underline the necessity for uniformity, if in nothing else, yet in the time taken by the rite. We laymen may not be busier than the clergy but we usually have much less choice in our hours of business. The celebrant who lengthens the service by ten minutes may, for us, throw the whole day into hurry and confusion. It is difficult to keep this out of our minds: it may even be difficult to avoid some feeling of resentment. Such temptations may be good for us but it is not the celebrant's business to supply them: God's permission and Satan's diligence will see to that part of our education without his assistance.

Secondly, I would ask the clergy to believe that we are more interested in orthodoxy and less interested in liturgiology as such than they can easily imagine. Dr Mascall rightly says that variations are permissible when they do not alter doctrine. But after that he goes on almost casually to mention "devotions to the Mother of God and to the hosts of heaven" as a possible liturgical variant. That the introduction of such devotions into any parish not accustomed to them would divide the congregation into two camps, Dr Mascall well knows. But if he thinks that the issue between those camps would be a liturgical issue, I submit that he is mistaken. It would be a doctrinal issue. Not one layman would be asking whether these devotions marred or mended the beauty of the rite; everyone would be asking whether they were lawful or damnable. It is no part of my object to discuss that question here, but merely to point out that it is the question.

What we laymen fear is that the deepest doctrinal issues should be tacitly and implicitly settled by what seem to be, or are avowed to be, merely changes in liturgy. A man who is wondering whether the fare set before him is food or poison is not reassured by being told that this course is now restored to its traditional place in the *menu* or that the tureen is of the Sarum pattern. We laymen are ignorant and timid. Our lives are ever in our hands, the avenger of blood is on our heels, and of each of us his soul may this night be required. Can you blame us if the reduction of grave doctrinal issues to merely liturgical issues fills us with something like terror?

(c) W.D.F. Hughes, ibid. (24th June 1949), p. 409

(d) C.S. Lewis, ibid. (1st July 1949), p. 427

Sir,

I agree with Dean Hughes that the connection of belief and liturgy is close, but doubt if it is "inextricable". I submit that the relation is healthy when liturgy expresses the belief of the Church, morbid when liturgy creates in the people by suggestion beliefs which the Church has not publicly professed, taught, and defended. If the mind of the Church is, for example, that our fathers erred in abandoning the Romish invocations of saints and angels, by all means let our corporate recantation, together with its grounds in scripture, reason and tradition be published, our solemn act of penitence be performed, the laity re-instructed, and the proper changes in liturgy be introduced.

What horrifies me is the proposal that individual priests should be encouraged to behave as if all this had been done when it has not been done. One correspondent compared such changes to the equally stealthy and (as he holds) irresistible changes in a language. But that is just the parallel that terrifies me, for even the shallowest philologist knows that the unconscious linguistic process is continually degrading good words and blunting useful distinctions. *Absit omen*! Whether an "enrichment" of liturgy which involves a change of doctrine is allowable, surely depends on whether our doctrine is changing from error to truth or from truth to error. Is the individual priest the judge of that?

(e) Edward Every, "Doctrine and Liturgy", ibid. (8th July 1949), pp. 445–6

(f) C.S. Lewis, "Invocation", ibid. (15th July 1949), pp. 463–4

Sir,

Mr Every (quite legitimately) gives the word *invocation* a wider sense than I. The question then becomes how far we can infer propriety of *devotion* from propriety of *invocation*? I accept the authority of the *Benedicite*[1] for the propriety of *invoking* (in Mr Every's sense) saints. But if I thence infer the propriety of *devotions* to saints, will not an argument force me to approve devotions to stars, frosts and whales?

I am also quite ready to admit that I overlooked a distinction. Our fathers might disallow a particular mediaeval doctrine and yet not disallow some other doctrine which we laymen easily confuse with it. But if the issue is so much finer than I thought, this merely redoubles my anxiety that it should be openly and authoritatively decided.

If I feared lest the suggestions of liturgy might beguile us laymen on a simple issue, I am not likely to be comforted by finding the issue a subtle one. If there is one kind of devotion to created beings which is pleasing and another which is displeasing to God, when is the Church, as a Church, going to instruct us in the distinction?

Meanwhile, what better opportunity for the stealthy insinuation of the wrong kind than the unauthorized and sporadic practice of devotions to creatures before uninstructed congregations would our ghostly foe desire? Most

---

[1] Found in the Prayer Book service of Morning Prayer, the original source of which is *The Song of the Three Holy Children* (vv. 35–66) in the old Testament Apocrypha

of us laymen, I think, have no *parti pris* in the matter. We desire to believe as the Church believes.

    (g) Edward Every "Invocation of Saints", ibid. (22nd July 1949), pp. 481–2

    (h) C.S. Lewis, ibid. (5th August 1949), p. 513

Sir,

I hope Mr Every has not misunderstood me. There is, I believe, a *prima facie* case for regarding devotions to saints in the Church of England as a controversial question (see Jewel, *Apologia Ecclesiae Anglicanae*, Pt. II, ch. xxviii, *Homilies*, Bk. II, *Peril of Idolatry*, Pt. III; Laud, *Conference with Fisher*, Sect. XXIII; Taylor, *Dissuasive from Popery*, Pt. I, ch. ii, sect. 8). I merely claim that the controversy exists. I share Mr Every's wish that it should cease. But there are two ways in which a controversy can cease: by being settled, or by gradual and imperceptible change of custom. I do not want any controversy to cease in the second way.

I implore priests to remember what Aristotle tells us about unconscious revolution (πολλάκις λανθάνει μεγάλη γινομένη μετάβασις τῶν νομίμων, *Politics* 1303 a 22).[1] When such unconscious revolution produces a result we like, we are all tempted to welcome it; thus I am tempted to welcome it when it leads to prayers for the dead. But then I see that the very same process can be used, and is used, to introduce modernist dilutions of the faith which, I am sure, Mr Every and I equally abominate. I conclude that a road so dangerous should never be trodden, whether the destination to which it seems to point is in itself good or bad.

---

[1] The occurrence of an important transition in customs often passes unnoticed

To write "No Thoroughfare" over that road is my only purpose.

8

The Holy Name

(a) Leslie E.T. Bradbury, "The Holy Name", *Church Times*, Vol. CXXXIV (3rd August 1951), p. 525

(b) C.S. Lewis, ibid. (10th August 1951), p. 541

Sir,

Having read Mr Bradbury's letter on the Holy Name, I have a few comments to make. I do not think we are entitled to assume that all who use this Name without reverential prefixes are making a "careless" use of it; otherwise, we should have to say that the Evangelists were often careless. I do not think we are entitled to assume that the use of the word *Blessed* when we speak of the Virgin Mary is "necessary"; otherwise, we should have to condemn both the Nicene and the Apostles' Creed for omitting it. Should we not rather recognize that the presence or absence of such prefixes constitute a difference, not in faith or morals, but simply in style? I know that as their absence is "irritating" to some, so their frequent recurrence is irritating to others. Is not each party innocent in its temperamental preference but grossly culpable if it allows anything so subjective, contingent, and (with a little effort) conquerable as a temperamental preference to become a cause of division among brethren? If we cannot lay down our tastes, along with other carnal baggage, at the church door, surely we should at least bring them in to be humbled and, if necessary, modified, not to be indulged?

9

Mere Christians

(a) R.D. Daunton-Fear, "Evangelical Churchmanship",
   Church Times, Vol. CXXXV (1st February 1952),
   p. 77

(b) C.S. Lewis, "Mere Christians", ibid. (8th February
   1952), p. 95

Sir,

I welcome the letter from the Rural Dean of Gravesend,
though I am sorry that anyone should have rendered it
necessary by describing the Bishop of Birmingham as an
Evangelical. To a layman, it seems obvious that what
unites the Evangelical and the Anglo-Catholic against the
"Liberal" or "Modernist" is something very clear and
momentous, namely, the fact that both are thoroughgoing
supernaturalists, who believe in the Creation, the Fall, the
Incarnation, the Resurrection, the Second Coming, and the
Four Last Things. This unites them not only with one
another, but with the Christian religion as understood
ubique et ab omnibus.[1]

The point of view from which this agreement seems less
important than their divisions, or than the gulf which
separates both from any non-miraculous version of Christianity, is to me unintelligible. Perhaps the trouble is that as
supernaturalists, whether "Low" or "High" Church, thus
taken together, they lack a name. May I suggest "Deep
Church"; or, if that fails in humility, Baxter's "mere Christians"?

[1] "everywhere and by all". See St Vincent of Lérins, *Commonitorium*, ii

10

Canonization

(a) Eric Pitt, "Canonization", *Church Times*, Vol. CXXXV (17th October 1952), p. 743

(b) C.S. Lewis, ibid. (24th October 1952), p. 763

Sir,

I am, like Mr Eric Pitt, a layman, and would like to be instructed on several points before the proposal to set up a "system" of Anglican canonization is even discussed. According to the *Catholic Encyclopaedia*, "saints" are dead people whose virtues have made them "worthy" of God's "special" love. Canonization makes *dulia* "universal and obligatory"; and, whatever else it asserts, it certainly asserts that the person concerned "is in heaven".

Unless, then, the word "canonization" is being used in a sense distinct from the Roman (and, if so, some other word would be much more convenient), the proposal to set up a "system" of canonization means that someone (say, the Archbishops) shall be appointed

(*a*) To tell us that certain named people are (i) "in heaven", and (ii) are "worthy" of God's "special" love.

(*b*) To lay upon us (under pain of excommunication?) the duty of *dulia* towards those they have named.

Now it is very clear that no one ought to tell us what he does not know to be true. Is it, then, held that God has promised (and, if so, when and where?) to the Church universal a knowledge of the state of certain departed souls? If so, is it clear that this knowledge will discern varying degrees of kinds of salvation such as are, I suppose, implicit in the word "special"? And if it does, will the promulgation of such knowledge help to save souls now *in viâ*? For it might well lead to a consideration of "rival claims", such as we read of in the *Imitation of Christ* (Bk. III, ch. 58), where we are warned, "Ask not which is greater in the Kingdom of Heaven . . . the search into such things brings no profit, but rather offends the saints themselves."

Finally, there is the practical issue: by which I do not mean the *Catholic Encyclopaedia's* neat little account of "the ordinary actual expenses of canonization" (though that too can be read with profit), but the danger of schism. Thousands of members of the Church of England doubt whether *dulia* is lawful. Does anyone maintain that it is necessary to salvation? If not, whence comes our obligation to run such frightful risks?

11

Pittenger-Lewis and *Version Vernacular*

(a) W. Norman Pittenger, "Pittenger-Lewis", *The Christian Century*, Vol. LXXV (24th December 1958), pp. 1485–6

(b) C.S. Lewis, "Version Vernacular", ibid. (31st December 1958), p. 515

Sir,

Thank you for publishing my "Rejoinder to Dr Pittenger" (26th November). Now would you, please, complete your kindness by publishing the statement that "*populam*" is either my typist's or your printer's error for "*populum*"?

An article on "translation" such as Dr Pittenger suggests

in his letter in the 24th December issue certainly needs doing, but I could not usefully do it for Americans. The vernacular into which they would have to translate is not quite the same as that into which I have translated. Small differences, in addressing proletarians, may be all-important.

In both countries an essential part of the ordination exam ought to be a passage from some recognized theological work set for translation into vulgar English – just like doing Latin prose. Failure on this paper should mean failure on the whole exam. It is absolutely disgraceful that we expect missionaries to the Bantus to learn Bantu but never ask whether our missionaries to the Americans or English can speak American or English. Any fool can write *learned* language. The vernacular is the real test. If you can't turn your faith into it, then either you don't understand it or you don't believe it.

12

Capital Punishment and *Death Penalty*

(a) C.S. Lewis, "Capital Punishment", *Church Times*, Vol. CXLIV (1st December 1961), p. 7

Sir,

I do not know whether capital punishment should or should not be abolished, for neither the natural light, nor scripture, nor ecclesiastical authority seems to tell me. But I am concerned about the grounds on which its abolition is being sought.

To say that by hanging a man we presumptuously judge him to be irredeemable is, I submit, simply untrue. My Prayer Book includes an exhortation to those under sentence of death which throughout implies the exact opposite. The real question is whether a murderer is more likely to repent and make a good end three weeks hence in the execution shed or, say, thirty years later in the prison infirmary. No mortal can know. But those who have most right to an opinion are those who know most by experience about the effect of prolonged prison life. I wish some prison chaplains, governors and warders would contribute to the discussion.

The suggestion of compensation for the relatives of the murdered man is in itself reasonable, but it ought not to be even remotely connected with the case for or against capital punishment. If it is, we shall be giving countenance to the archaic, and surely erroneous, view that murder is primarily an offence not against society but against individuals.

Hanging is not a more irrevocable act than any other. You can't bring an innocent man to life: but neither can you give him back the years which wrongful imprisonment has eaten.

Other correspondents have pointed out that a theory of punishment which is purely exemplary or purely reformatory, or both, is shockingly immoral. Only the concept of desert connects punishment with morality at all. If deterrence is all that matters, the execution of an innocent man, provided the public think him guilty, would be fully justified. If reformation alone is in question, then there is nothing against painful and compulsory reform for all our defects, and a Government which believes Christianity to be a neurosis will have a perfectly good right to hand us all over to their straighteners for "cure" tomorrow.

(b) Claude Davis, ibid. (8th December 1961), p. 14

(c) C.S. Lewis, "Death Penalty", ibid. (15th December 1961), p. 12

Sir,

Mr Davis rightly reproves me for using the word *society* as I did. This hypostatized abstraction has already done harm enough. But I only meant "all of us". The absurdity of the view which treats murder as an offence against a single family is best illustrated in the case in the private speeches of Demosthenes (I can't turn it up at the moment, but your more scholarly readers no doubt can).[1]

A man, *A*, set free a female slave, *B*, his old nurse. *B* married. Her husband died without issue. Someone then murdered *B*. But under Athenian law no one could prosecute because there was no injured party. *A* could not act because *B*, when murdered, was no longer his property. There was no widower, and there were no orphans.

I am on neither side in the present controversy. But I still think the abolitionists conduct their case very ill. They seem incapable of stating it without imputing vile motives to their opponents. If unbelievers often look at your correspondence column, I am afraid they may carry away a bad impression of our logic, manners and charity.

---

[1] *The Orations of Demosthenes*, "The Oration against Euergus and Mnesibulus," sections 1155–62